First/Only

First/Only

Nedson W. Campbell

FIRST/ONLY

iUniverse books may be ordered through booksellers or by contacting:

iUniverse LLC
1663 Liberty Drive
Bloomington, IN 47403
www.iuniverse.com
1-800-Authors (1-800-288-4677)

Because of the dynamic nature of the Internet, any web addresses or links contained in this book may have changed since publication and may no longer be valid. The views expressed in this work are solely those of the author and do not necessarily reflect the views of the publisher, and the publisher hereby disclaims any responsibility for them.

Any people depicted in stock imagery provided by Thinkstock are models, and such images are being used for illustrative purposes only.
Certain stock imagery © Thinkstock.

ISBN: 978-1-4917-0026-6 (sc)
ISBN: 978-1-4917-0028-0 (hc)
ISBN: 978-1-4917-0027-3 (e)

Library of Congress Control Number: 2013913687

Printed in the United States of America

iUniverse rev. date: 07/10/2014

Preface

The old saying goes "FIRST THINGS FIRST". From the beginning of time the word "First" or "Only" has always been a part of our daily lives. People are always trying to be First or being then only person to achieve the unthinkable.

The one sentence most often used upon meeting someone for the first time is, "What's you name," or "How do you do" or "First let me welcome you".

In the Bible the first murder committed was when Cain killed his brother Able. It's still a mystery as to what weapon was used or who witnessed the act. The rivalry of significance may have started in High School. Who came in first at graduation or who came first or who was the only person at school to break a record on the track or football field. But it is also mentioned that the first top ten graduates of the class do not normally succeed or become better off than the second ten in the class. Then again the person who is placed <u>LAST</u> can also be glory to fame. West Point graduates are all Lieutenants and received the same pay upon graduation. The cadet who graduates first and makes the military a career most likely will make the rank of General. Old tradition dictates that the person who comes <u>LAST</u> in the class receives <u>ONE DOLLAR</u> from the other graduates.

Adventures are always mentioned as people who successfully become the first to go solo around the world, flew the first plane at the speed of sound or crossed the ocean alone using just sails or oars. Sir Edmund Hillary was the first to reach the peak of

Mount Everest. But people still say his Sherpa, Tenzing Norgay may have been first. There's no photo of Sir Edmud at the top. Anyway, we will never know because Norgay is dead and I don't think Sir Hillary would change history.

This book will set the records straight as to who or what was First or Only. It will make a good debate for students to discuss the Only people. First will always be First.

Hopefully as always this book "FIRST/ONLY" is extremely informative and sometimes humorous.

Thank You

First I want to thank all of my friends and all the other good people that patronized my efforts with my first try "Where Do You Get That From?". I also want to thank all the people that gave me encouragement to write another book.

A special THANK YOU to Stephanie Avello who did a great job with the typing and corrections. At times I thought she was getting tired of me.

My children who are a good source of daily encouragement and laughter are all grown and have moved on to seeking fame and fortune in far-away places. Jeanelle is now living in California working as a Project Coordinator for an eating disorder facility. Edward earned his Ph.D. in alternative medicine and is also living in California. N.J., now (2013) in his last year of internship at Yale University will next be moving into his fellowship in Psychiatry. We give them all our blessing and support.

First/Only

The Guidestar navigation system is ONLY the first generation of devices that one day will likely be as common as car radios.

The first major museum dedicated to the Underground Railroad—the National Underground Railroad Freedom Center—was opened in the year 2002 in Cincinnati, Ohio.

Little Richard's first hit, "Tutti Frutti" coincided with Rosa Park's letting the white folks know she would not be forced to sit in the rear of a public bus, thus launching the civil rights movement.

Lexus presented the worlds first in dash, six-disc CD Auto-Changer.

In 1996 the West Indian Carnival (Brooklyn Carnival) was televised locally for the first time. London's Notting Hill Carnival is now Europe's largest cultural festival, with millions of participants representing almost every race and creed.

Stanley H. Greene is president of the BOX-USA, the worlds first and ONLY interactive music video cable channel.

It was in Bristol, Pa where the first aircraft company merger took place, when the Loenig Company merged with Keystone. It was also in Bristol where Fleetwings Aircraft set up shop in 1934 and built the U.S. first all-stainless steel aircraft, the amphibious Sea Bird.

Sgt. Danyell Wilson is the first Black female guard at the Tomb of the Unknown Soldiers at Arlington National Cemetery. Wilson is a member of the Old Guard, the official ceremonial unit of the U.S. Army.

Israel L. Gaither is the new chief secretary of the Salvation Army-USA Eastern territory. Gaither is the first African-American and the youngest ever appointed to this position.

ONLY once in the 50-year history of the College World Series has the game ended with a homerun, (in '96 when Warren Morris' two-run, bottom-of-the-ninth shot won the title for LSU).

Not ONLY was GRAPE IV the first teraflop supercomputer ever built, but also its simulations of small globular clusters confirmed Sugimoto's theory that the cores of these clusters oscillate.

In 1949, the first Russian atomic bomb was tested.

September 18, 1999 marked the 100th anniversary of the first fatal auto accident in the United States. It happened at 51st and Lexington Avenue in NYC.

Female mosquitoes lay their eggs ONLY in water.

January 2000 Senator Ben Nighthorse Campbell chairman of the Senate Indian Affairs Committee is the ONLY American Indian in the U.S. Senate.

Although Ehud Barak was not the first Israeli leader to visit the Sachsenhausen concentration camp near Berlin, he was the first since Germany reclaimed the one-time sear of Nazi power as it's capital.

If you put the 400 richest Americans together (in the year 2000) their fortunes would hit the $1 Trillion mark for the first time-that's greater than the gross domestic product of China.

Yemen's first direct presidential election was marred by low turnout on September 23rd, 1999.

Consider Raw Vanilla the very first men's fragrance to feature vanilla as its star ingredient.

The first-time procedure of an ovarian implant appears to have restored fertility to a menopausal woman.

For the first time, injections of the hormone leptin has been shown to curb appetite and induce weight loss in a human.

Pedro Almodovar of Spain is not ONLY among the world's most famous directors, but probably the ONLY living foreign-language filmmaker whose name alone can sell movies in the U.S.

Sir Edmund Hillary, the British adventurer led the first expedition to the South Pole.

(9/16/99) caused severe flood warning in Philadelphia and it's surrounding area for the first time ever, (excessive rain due to Hurricane Floyd). At Temple University 5.38" of rain fell in one day, a record.

During WWII the Japanese submarine I-52 was sunk by U.S. pilots—in the U.S. the mission was heralded as the first coordinated kill of a submarine using sonobuoys and acoustic torpedoes.

The Denver schools have become the first big-city U.W. school district to approve a contract that links teacher pay to student performance.

The downing of the F117A on March 27, 1999 in Yugoslavia was the first loss of a stealth aircraft in combat.

With Senator Beverly Hollingsworth's' election as Senate president September 99', New Hampshire became the first state to have a female governor, a female Senate president and a female House Speaker all at the same time.

The first Farm Aid concert was held in 1985; the host and chief organizer was and still is Willie Nelson.

The 737 is the ONLY commercial jet with a rudder (the largest moving part of the jet) controlled by a single hydraulic valve. Other jets have multiple valves that can compensate for each other if one jams.

The first democratic transfer of power in Russia's history took place on May 7th, 2000 with President Vladimir Putin pledged to finish building democracy and restore the country to it's world power status.

Doctors performed the first operation September 23, 1998 (replacing a hand on a patient) in Lyons, France and the second one in Louisville, Kentucky. First person in the world was Clint Hallman an Australian, the second person and first American was Nathan Scott.

In 1997 physicians at Vanderbilt University Medical Center in Nashville, Tennessee, successfully performed the first fetal surgery for a nonlethal disorder called spina bifida.

In April '91, with the conclusion of the NBA regular season, financially strapped franchises can, for the first time, apply for assistance from the league.

The Converse All-Starr He:01 is the first shoe to use lighter-than-air helium as a cushion.

A Wildlife Conservation Society biologist first glimpsed the world's smallest (25 lbs) deer in Burma in 1997.

Virgil Foster was believed to be the first person in California killed in an attack of "killer" bees, and sixth nationwide. Foster was a beekeeper.

Disney World in Florida was forced to close its operations for the first time ever on September 14, 1999. Hurricane Floyd with winds of up to 145 mph was the cause.

In 1990 Ashanthi DeSilva became the world's first patient to receive gene therapy. Doctors injected the girl with a healthy gene that produces an infection-fighting enzyme.

In the 1950', Wistar's Leonard Hayflick and Paul S. Moorhead grew the first normal human cell line in a culture dish—an important step in the development of vaccines and the manufacturing of human aging.

The world's first digital computer weighed 30 tons. Nauchly and co-inventor J. Presper Echert, then at Penn, later founded the company that became Unisys.

When American Forests began cataloguing in 1917, creating America's first National Register of Big Trees, it was an act of preservation.

In 1983, Drexel University in Philadelphia, Pa became the U.S. first university to require every student to have personal access to a microcomputer.

Cay Burns is the first woman commander of the Liberty Bell Chapter of American ex-POW's.

Cuauhtemoc Cardenas, son of revered former President of Mexico Lazaro Cardenas, is the first elected mayor of Mexico City, the most prominent figure on Mexico's left.

Lynette Woodard, a former University of Kansas star who is the all-time leading scorer in NCAA women's basketball, became the first woman to join the Harlem Globetrotters basketball team in 1985.

The MOMSENG LUNG invented by Swede Momsen in '39 was the first self-contained breathing device for human use underwater-which opened the way for modern scuba diving.

On June 9, 1902 Horn & Hardart opened the first automat restaurant in America in Philadelphia, Pa.

The U. S. first Thanksgiving Day Parade presented by Gimbels in Philadelphia, Pa, November 25, 1920.

The first Pennsylvania lottery ticket was sold March 7, 1972.

Bishop John Neumann was canonized June 19, 1977-thus becoming the first male American Saint.

The ONLY perennial best-sellers ever penned in Philadelphia are the Declaration of Independence and the Constitution.

Judith Rodin, a 1966 graduate of the University of Pennsylvania became its first female president-the first female president of any Ivy League School, for that matter.

President Jimmy Carter named the first black woman cabinet member-Secretary of Housing and Urban Development Patricia R. Harris.

The 79-year-old Miss America Organization held the Miss America pageant at the Convention Hall in Atlantic City, N.J. accomplished a lot of FIRSTS during the crowning of Miss America 2000:

First time a host woman (Marie Osmond) announces another woman as winner, Heather Renee French. First time in the history of the pageant that a Miss America comes from the state of Kentucky. For the first time, contestants provided all their own outfits. Two-piece swimsuits were allowed but no thongs. The first tremor came when pageant officials quietly tried to change next year's eligibility rules to allow Candidates who had been married or pregnant, and had an abortion or a child who died. Heather Renee French became the first Miss America to wear the newly designed Rhinestone-and-ruby "Millennium" Crown.

Gabrielle Kirk McDonald is the ONLY American who is also black-among 14 judges of the International Criminal Tribunal for the former Yugoslavia.

Frenchman Fabrice Gropaiz braved the wind-whipped tundra of Siberia and the baked canyon lands of Northern Mexico (among some 15 countries) to become the first person to circumnavigate the globe on skates.

Aretha Franklin "Queen of Soul"-was the first woman inducted in Rock 'N Roll Hall of Fame.

Air Force Col. Eileen Collins became the first female to be commander of a space shuttle flight. Space shuttle Columbia released the worlds most powerful x-ray telescope weighing the heaviest ever on a shuttle flight.

A Pyrenean mountain dog has become the first pet since 1901 to enter Britain without the rigid six-month quarantine period.

ONLY Sandy Koufax (4) and Bob Feller (3) have more than two no-hitters compared to 7 by Nolan Ryan.

Casual "Cal" Dupree and his partner Cedric "Ricky" Walker, founders and owners of the Universal Big Top Circus, b-boys, with Black aerialists broke ground in '94 for African-Americans. The ONLY other documented African-American owned circus was started by a man named Efram Lewis over 100 years ago.

Although the first all Black movie channel has been on select cable airwaves since February '97, if you don't live in certain parts of Louisiana, D.C. or California, you'll be on a never ending quest for your 24-hour melanted film experience.

Since 1953, when REM (rapid eye movement), or the dream state, was first recognized, about thirty studies have dissected gender differences in dreaming.

ONLY two players other than Michael Jordon have averaged 30 points a game at age 30 or older—Jerry West and Rick Barry.

ONLY three fillies have won the Kentucky Derby:

> Regret (1915) Genuine Rick (1980) and Winning Colors (1988).

Johannes Brahms finished his first symphony in 1876 at age 42.

Japanese women were able to buy contraceptive pills in 1999 for the first time. Americans had it 40 years ago.

Hockey Hall of Famer Mario Lemieux opened new territory for modern-day millionaire athletes by becoming the first ex-player to embrace the role as decision-making owner of a major pro sports franchise.

When James Hormel, the first openly gay U.S. ambassador takes up his post in Luxembourg in September '99 it will be in one of the world's most tolerant societies-or in a country five centuries behind the times.

Hunters crossing a glacier in northern Canada have discovered the well preserved frozen body of an early American (August '99) the first "iceman" found in North America.

Cypress Hill, The Offspring and No Doubt are among the performers slated for the first ARTIST direct Online Music Awards, October 7th, 1999 at the House of Blues in Los Angeles.

British band Blor says it will record the first music to be played on Mars. The group volunteered to write a song to be beamed back from the Red Planet when the unmanned British space probe Beagle 2 lands there in 2003.

Rock legend Van Morrison is set to become the first star inducted into Dublin's Irish Music Hall of Fame.

In September '99 Major General David Hale became the first U.S. Army general to be demoted in 45 years.

North and South Korea naval ships exchanged fire June 15, 1999 at the disputed Yellow Sea Border in the first such skirmish since the end of the 1950-1953 Korean War.

The Douglas Skyraider was the U.S. Navy's first jet fighter.

The first Monday in October is traditionally the starting date of the U. S. Supreme Court term.

ONLY four percent (4%) of all veterans service-connected disability claims are given approval.

ONLY about one third to half of the world's people regularly sit down in a chair.

Haverford, Pennsylvania (near Philadelphia) is the ONLY College in the U.S. that still awards a letter in varsity cricket.

Before tossing out the first ball at the 1986 World Series, Speaker of the House, Tip O'Neill practiced for two weeks in a Capital hallway. He threw a perfect strike.

Andrew Akers and Dwane van der Sluis of New Zealand set up the first Zorb venue (is a transparent, inflatable plastic ball within a ball) in Rotorua, New Zealand, in 1996, the Kiwi craze has spread to Europe and South Africa.

ONLY one in five adult Americans considers him or herself computer literate.

There are ONLY about four (4) thousand words in the English sign, but over 40 thousand words in the English Language.

The ONLY woman to receive the Medal of Honor of all the recipients was Dr. Mary Edwards Walker.

ONLY five percent (5%) of babies are born on their due date.

The ONLY thing a virus cannot penetrate is glass.

The first U.S. Presidential car was one seized from Al Capone and used by President Truman. The car was armor plated.

The first 24-hour 7-Eleven store opened in 1963 in Las Vegas, Nevada.

When President Bill Clinton took office in 1992 there was ONLY one chartered school in the U. S. At the beginning of the school year in '99 there were over 1700.

Viagra works for ONLY seventy percent (70%) of patients.

ONLY sixteen percent (16%) of Israeli Jews define themselves as religious.

In 1995 Soo Yeun Kim was honored as a finalist in the Westinghouse Science Talent Search, the first time this award was made posthumously.

The first covered bridge in America was built by Timothy Palmera, a Massachusetts carpenter. The bridge was located in Philadelphia, spanning the Schuykill River.

Television ABC's Wide World of Sports was first aired on April 29, 1961 with host Jim McKay.

Bill Irwin does not give up easily, in November 1990 he became the first blind person known to have walked the entire Appalachian Trail.

On January 2, 1996 Officer Lauretha (Laurie) Vaird, a Mother of two boys was killed, Vaird became the first Philadelphia policewoman to be slain in the line of duty.

McDonald's first mascot was named "Speedy".

On Sunday September 12, 1999 was be the first time that Iraq chairs the Arab League of Foreign Ministers since the invasion of Kuwait.

The Chicago Military Academy opened August '99 as the first public school in the United States run by the Army's Junior Reserve Officer Training Corps (JROTC)

The 8th Regiment Armory is in the city of Chicago, once home to the U.S. first black commanded infantry unit.

The Old Testament is first of all the sacred Bible of Judaism, and it is so regarded at the present time.

The Johnson Sea Link submersible plunged 3,000 feet beneath the surface as history's first deep-diving expedition to the Galapagos probes depths where no camera has gone before.

Teotihuacán, the first metropolis in the Western Hemisphere, lies about 25 miles from Mexico City.

Meriwether Lewis and William Clark (Lewis and Clark), exploring the new Louisiana Purchase, forging to the Pacific and back in three years (1804-1806), they were the first Americans to see the entire sweep of the continent.

The Galapagos worms marked the first discovery of living things that used chemical energy rather than relying on the sun for energy.

For the first time since 1980, three teen-agers advanced to the women's semi-finals at the 1999 U.S Open—Martina Hingis, Venus Williams and her sister Serena Williams.

Theodore Roosevelt was the first U.S. President to have his life chronicled on film.

Vancouver, Canada was the first foreign visit by Bill Clinton when he became President. Since becoming President, Clinton has traveled more miles than Ronald Reagan and George Bush combined.

Although our fingers and toes are fused when they first form in the womb, we emerge without webbing because the cells that join our digits die.

The Triple A Calgary Cannons hit three grand slams in one game (May '91), it's believed to be the first time a pro team at any level has done that.

Connie Whitener Perdreau, the study-abroad coordinator at Ohio University, is the first Black president of NAFSA: Association of International Educators, the world's largest professional association devoted to international educational exchanges.

Marjorie M. Brown is Atlanta's first female postmaster and one of ONLY two women in the nation to head a major city post office.

The Sacramento district attorneys dropped charges against Robert De Arkland for growing medical marijuana. The seized plants were not watered and they died. De Arkland sued his homeowner's insurance company and won-thus becoming the first known instances in the U.S. in which an insurer has paid for losses of medical marijuana.

William C. Dement, MD., founded the world's first known sleep-disorders clinic at Stanford University and has practiced sleep medicine for the past three decades.

The Leica was the first commercially successful miniature camera that accepted the 35mm film.

ONLY three kinds of regular polygons (straight-edged figures whose edges are all the same length and whose angles are all the same) can be fitted together side-by-side to cover a plane: equilateral triangles, squares and regular hexagons. Others will leave gaps.

ABC programming executive Jamie Tarses was the first woman to serve as programming president at one of the three (i.e. ABC, NBC & CBS) major broadcast networks.

Larry LaBan, the dry-cleaning man, went into the bird business with Colonel Harland D. Sanders, becoming Michigan's first Kentucky Fried Chicken franchisee.

Denmark's first royal birth in 24 years, Prince Joachim and wife Princess Alexandra had a boy August 28, 1999.

The octagonal school house built in the early 1900's near the corner of Big Oak and Oxford Valley Roads, Bucks County, Pennsylvania was the first octagonal school house in the United States.

ONLY when water droplets reach a certain size can they fall toward the ground and become drops of rain.

In the desert east of Los Angeles in the sand dunes you'll find the tiny Delhi Sands flower-loving fly, the ONLY fly ever to make the Endangered Species List.

Number of grand slams completed by Rod Laver (2 in 1962 and 1969) at the U.S. Championships, making him the ONLY player to accomplish the feat twice.

Since 1898, Campbell Soup Company has ONLY made 14 minor changes to the red-and-white label. The last change was made for select varieties in 1994 to mark the Company's 125th anniversary.

Under the Fair Credit Billing Act, you are ONLY responsible for $50.00, and most card issuers won't hold you responsible for any amount, as long as you report the problem right away.

There have ONLY been about 200 attempts to separate conjoined twins in medical history, and there are enough different types of conjoined twins that there is no way to give a percentage chance of survival in a given case.

Instant replay made its first appearance in the NFL from 1986-91, and was deemed a failure because it interrupted the flow of games without yielding a significant number of overturned calls.

The presidential news conference is the ONLY forum in our society where the U.S. President can be questioned.

During the Nixon administration Helen Thomas became the first female Chief of the UPI Bureau at the White House. Helen was 78 years old when she resigned when the "Moonies" bought UPI during the Bill Clinton administration in May 2000.

The event that made high school a universal experience was the Great Depression. The first year in which a majority of high school-age individuals were enrolled in high school was 1932.

El Cenizo, Texas is believed to be the ONLY U.S. city with an all-Spanish policy. English translations of meetings are available but must be requested 48 hours in advance.

The giant panda is native ONLY to China.

Despite their decades-long relationship Britain's Prince Charles and longtime love Camille Parker-Bowles appeared together in public for the first time in June '99.

Bertrand Piccard, a psychiatrist and co-pilot Brian Jones in a balloon called Breitling Orbiter 3 became the first two people to successfully circle the globe non-stop in a balloon. They carried a teddy bear that became the first bear to circle the globe in a balloon, the journey lasted 20 days (March 1-21, 1999).

ONLY one African-American chose to enroll in '97 at the University of California law school—Proposition 209 and anti-affirmative action comrades on the VC's Board of Regents have made it difficult for people of color to gain entrance to the system.

Adrian IV is the ONLY Pope from England.

The first military (August '99) exercise between Japan and South Korea took place in the East China Sea between Japan's Southwestern island of Kyushu and South Korea's Cheju Island.

The annual Regatta race in Newfoundland, Canada, began for the first time (August '99) with women racers, this is a first in 173 years as there are more women (75%) racers than men.

In 1931, an organic chemist and priest named Julius Nieunland invented the first synthetic rubber, neoprene marketed by DuPont as Duprene.

Tim, a 75 pound golden retriever served as the first puppy in flight training for Guide Dogs for the Blind.

Allie B. Latimer, now retired after a career in private practice and with the (GSA) General Services Administration, she was the first black woman to serve as General Counsel (lawyer) for a Federal Agency.

Hillary Clinton was the first person to grace the cover of the first issue of "Talk" magazine.

ONLY one of 20 prospective drugs passing the test-tube test makes it into the market from the U.S. Army Medical Research Institute of Infectious Diseases in Fort Detrick, MD.

Captain Kathryn Sullivan was the first woman to walk in space.

The first female host of Saturday Night Live was Candice Bergan ("Miss Murphy Brown").

The ONLY natural resource Israel has is water, which is becoming a rare commodity in the Middle East. Water is getting so scarce that it's becoming more important than oil.

Former Beatle John Lennon was the first person to appear on the cover of "Rolling Stones" magazine.

Fluoride is the ONLY medication taken by children (including babies) and adults without anyone controlling the dosage.

The Franklin Half Dollar minted from 1948-1963, is the first circulated U.S. coin to immortalize someone other than a president.

John Siney founded the first anthracite coal miners' union, the Workingman's Benevolent Association in 1868.

When the Johnson Publishing Company vice president and agency director, Willie Miles Burns, died in March '96 she was remembered by her cousin Ebony Publisher John H. Johnson as one of the first women executives of a nation magazine.

Among the roaring engines of military transport planes, a team of 13 U.S. Marines walked across a runway in Australia September 18, 1999, the first to arrive in a contingent of American forces that will participate in an international mission in East Timor.

For the first time since 1976, Pennsylvania has replaced about 9 million yellow and blue license plates through June 2002. The new plates are the first in the world to feature a Web-Site address, www.state.pa.us, the states official home page.

Raisa Gorbachev, wife of the last Soviet President Mikhail Gorbachev was the first wife of any Soviet President to publicly use and own an American Express Credit Card.

Captain Deborah McCoy will supervise more than 5,200 pilots and 8,700 flight attendants as Continental Airlines Senior Vice President of flight operations, the first such appointment in the U.S. by a major airline.

NASA's Liberty Bell-7 space capsule that splashed down with Gus Grissom on July 21, 1961 is the ONLY U.S. manned spacecraft lost after a successful mission.

Dorothy Dandridge is best known for two movie musicals, Porgy and Bess and Carmen Jones for which she was nominated for an Oscar for Best Actress in 1955—the first African-American actress to accomplish this feat.

The U.S. Coast Guard honored Alex Haley (7/10/99), Pulitzer Prize winning author of "Roots" by commissioning a cutter in his name—the first military vessel named for a journalist. Haley served 20 years in the Coast Guard.

In May 1998 the people of London, England (population 7 million) were allowed to choose their mayor for the first time.

In the fall of '99 the first Singapore film "That's the Way I Like It" was shown in the U.S.

A crowd swarmed the tiny central village in Quang Tri (August '99) province of Vietnam to mark the 200th anniversary of a sighting of an apparition of the Virgin Mary, the ONLY one reported in Southeast Asia.

Steve Forbes, the millionaire publisher came in second behind George W. Bush in the 1999 Iowa Straw Poll for the Republican race. He had the ONLY air conditioned tent during the rally.

The Rev. J. Bryan Hehir, a Roman Catholic priest, was named as head of the 183 year old Harvard Divinity School (August '99) making him the first Catholic to assume the post in a permanent capacity.

ONLY five percent (5%) of the U.S. 2 billion acre landmass, excluding Alaska, is considered developed, according to a 1996 statistical abstract of the U.S. Department of Commerce.

A half century ago, Chinese and South Korean soldiers faced each other on the battlefield in North Korea. In 1999 for the first time ever, the commanders of the two militaries faced each other in the conference room.

The SWAT team in Rio de Janeiro, Brazil is the ONLY one in the world trained to shoot from a flying helicopter while hanging from outside.

An Oregon college student (Jeffrey Levy, 22) pleaded guilty to illegally distributing thousands of pirated software programs, movies and pieces of music from his Web Site, giving the government its first Internet-piracy conviction under a 1997 law.

The bar code—that ubiquitous and unfathomable collection of lines and numbers made its debut for the first time in 1974. Starting in 2005, the codes will be redesigned to use 13 and 14 digits, up from 10 numbers.

The first bank (G&L Bank-the initials stands for gay and lesbian) to target a national homosexual market has opened its doors in Pensacola, Florida and began doing business October 11, 1999

In 2004 at the Summer Olympics in Greece for the first time in 76 years there was a major new design on the medals.

The first time the public demonstrated against the Mafia was when Sicily's Judge Giovanni Falcone and his wife, also a judge, died in 1992 when a ton of dynamite blew up their bulletproof car.

The Cadillac DeVille is the first car to offer night-vision technology—comes with On Star Communication system.

Nobel Prize in medicine Hamilton Smith discovered the first tools for dissecting DNA, the stuff from which all life springs.

ONLY about one in three firms with foreign owners or investors in China posted a profit in 1993.

Akio Morita and fellow engineer Masaru Ibuka (Sony Corporation founders) produced Japan's first magnetic recoding tape and tape recorder in 1950. Morita was also the ONLY non-American on U.S. based Time magazine's list of top 19 businessmen of the 20th century.

The grand unveiling of the $70 million, seven month restoration of Radio City Music Hall in New York City occurred on October 4, 1999. It was the first major renovation of the building since it opened December 27, 1932.

Elizabeth Diller and Ricardo Scofidio, the first architects to win a MacArthur "genius grant", also deal in earthier matters.

Pamela Rosenberg was appointed general director of the San Francisco Opera, which made her the ONLY woman heading an opera company in the U.S. (A/O1999)

Aspirin was first developed in 1897 to relieve arthritis-people consume 45,000 tons of aspirin around the world.

The first military rabbi was Jacob Frankel, the 54 year old leader of Rodeph Shalom Congregation in Philadelphia.

Martha Roundtree, pioneering journalist who co-created NBC's Meet the Press, TV's longest running program also started radio's first panel show, Leave It to the Girls.

The federal government of Canada for the first time gave permission for the cultivation and use of marijuana for medical purposes in June 1999.

Montgomery Ward's first catalogue was ONLY one page.

Edgar Allan Poe at 18 published his first volume of poetry "Tamerlane and Other Poems" anonymously. Poe was "the first literary author many people read, the first great writer".

A vice dean of John Hopkins University School of Medicine was named on October 8, 1999 as editor of the American Medical Association's influential journal, making her the first female editor in its 116 year history.

Senator John McCain, '99 U.S. GOP presidential candidate's father and grandfather were both four star generals in the U.S. Navy and ONLY father to father four star.

The laboratory of cell biology at Rockefeller University bio-medical research institute ONLY accepts graduate students and grants ONLY doctorates.

During the Boer War (October 1899-1902) the British herded about 25,000 blacks and 94,000 whites—most of them family members of Boer Commandoes-into the world's first concentration camps.

The great 482 year dispute between Catholics and Protestants came to an end when 2003 Representatives of Pope John Paul II and the Lutheran World Federation met in Ausburg, Germany to sign a theological declaration that salvation comes ONLY through faith in God. This is the first authoritative declaration the Catholic Church has taken with any of the Reformation Churches.

Saint Louis is the ONLY King of France to be canonized.

Vanguard Group, the U.S. second largest mutual fund firm was the first fund company to disclose after-tax returns on a broad range of mutual funds.

Paul Cayard became the first skipper in 1998 to win the Whitbread Round the World Race.

Angela Davis, the longtime leftist, philosophy professor at the University of California Santa Cruz campus, is the ONLY member of her faculty to have made the FBI's 10 Most Wanted List.

In 1999 Notah Begay II was the ONLY American Indian playing on the U.S. PGA Tour. Begay, whose first name means "almost there" in Navajo.

Isaac Grainger, the former president of the U.S. Golf Association (USGA) presented Arnold Palmer with his first amateur champion cup in 1954.

In studies using macaque monkeys, the researchers at Princeton University have for the first time traced the path followed by neurons that are created in one part of the brain and then migrate to the neocortex, the center of the minds ability to reason and think.

Male mosquitoes feed ONLY on nectar not humans.

Cincinnati has appealed the dismissal (lawsuit 10/7/99) against firearms manufacturers, which demanded reimbursement for the costs of providing police emergency, court and prison services for shootings. It was the first dismissed of a suit brought against gun makers by a municipality.

The first Medal of Honor was presented in 1863 to a Union Army private, Jacob Parrott.

The first modern personality test, the Woodworth Personal Data Sheet of 1919, was designed to help the U.S. Army screen out recruits who might be susceptible to shell shock.

As for the idea of personal space, it was not until the 1700 in England that corridors were first included in the home of the well-to-do. Until then, to get from room A to room E, one had to walk through all the rooms in between.

William H. Bechler, America's first umbrella company, long gone, was headquartered in Philadelphia, Pennsylvania.

United Airlines, the U.S. largest, was the first to make the decision on July 30, 1999 that they would extend employee benefits to homosexuals, followed closely by American and US Airways.

Encyclopedia Britannica became the first encyclopedia available on the Web in 1994, but there was an $85-a-year subscription fee.

U.S. District Judge William H. Walls is the first federal judge to reject the government's longstanding practice of detaining or deporting immigrants based on evidence it refuses to share, lawyers who follow immigration say.

For the first time (January 1, 2000) since Theodore Roosevelt used the gunboat diplomacy to wrest the Isthmus of Panama from Colombia and create a special-purpose state where the United States could build and run the canal, Panamanians are on their own.

Surnames (last names), did not emerge until the mid 1300's. Before then men typically were identified ONLY by the names of their fathers—John, son of Henry' Martin, Peter's son—and women took the names of their fathers or husbands.

Cuba said that the visit (10/23/99) of a U.S. governor, Republican Illinois Governor George Ryan was the first since Fidel Castro took power in 1959.

In its first ever referendum on Roe vs. Wade, the Senate went on record as saying the landmark abortion ruling established an important constitutional right and should not be overturned.

His son put a mighty scare into his No.1 team, but Bobby Bowden sneaked away with career win No. 300. Florida State rallied for a 17-14 victory over Clemson October 23, 1999 in major college football's first father vs. son coaching matchup—Tommy Bowden, son.

Modern human beings first appeared about 100,000 years ago, but they were extremely few in number and very widely dispersed.

"First things first".

Airlifting the frozen hulk of the world's first intact mammoth carcass to the Siberian town of Khatanga, the team of Paleontologists said their find could lead to a breakthrough in cloning an animal that has been extinct for 10,000 years.

In 1999 there were ONLY about 300 white whales still swimming the Atlantic, researchers say. The population was thinned out decades ago by whalers who killed them for their thick blubber and baleen.

Bob Smith, a retired biologist agreed to pay a record $19,000 for the privilege of adopting a 6 month old Kiger mustang horse at the first Kiger mustang auction.

Founded in 1927, ONLY Woody Allen and dancer Rudolf Nureyev were allowed to wear hats inside the original Russian Tea Room (RTR) a legendary spot for New York Celebrities.

The specially outfitted LC-130 transport is the ONLY large plane in the world meant to fly in and out of the Pole.

Lights! Cameras! and Action!, for Milton Berle and Sid Caesar as they were honored on October 25, 1999 as the first inductees in NBC's walk of fame.

Cliff Bayer's victory was the first ever by an American duelist (fencing) in any discipline—foil, epee or saber—at the World Championship level. Fencing has traditionally been an Old World sport dominated by Europeans who devote their lives to it.

In 1842 Alexander Cartwright helped start the first organized baseball club.

Eugeniusz Koczuk, the owner of an import company called Gino International, and his associate Wieslaw Rozbick are the first people to be prosecuted under new provisions in the Convention on International Trade in Endangered Species.

It wasn't until 1898 when the Photographic Society of Philadelphia, the U.S. oldest camera club, teamed up with the Pennsylvania Academy of the Fine arts to host a series of exhibitions called the Philadelphia Photographic Salons. The Salons became the U.S. first artistic photo display juried by professionals.

Space Imaging Inc. released the first commercially available high resolution satellite images in October 1999, showing Washington, D. C.

A panel of federal judges in October 1999 overturned the death sentence of a man who was the first person sentenced to execution by the U.S. under a 1988 federal drug law.

Rev. Leon Sullivan, the pastor of Philadelphia's Zion Baptist Church, Sullivan helped found the city's first shopping center built and owned by blacks, and also became the first black man to sit on the board at General Motors.

Dr. David Banner, better known as "The Incredible Hulk" was one of the first TV characters to have identity problems. (When he got angry—really angry—the normally mild-mannered doctor, played Bill Bixby.)?

In a radical new view of pre-history, two prominent archeologists say North America's first inhabitants may have crossed the icy Atlantic Ocean some 18,000 years ago from Europe's Iberian Peninsula.

A scouting troop (the 129th Toronto Scouting Group) for gay and lesbian young adults has been set up in Toronto, apparently the first of its kind in North America.

The NASDAQ composite index vaulted to its fourth straight closing high 11/3/99, finishing above 3,000 for the first time ever.

By a margin of 62 percent to 38 percent, San Francisco voters outlawed the $1.00 and $2.00 fees that banks charge non-account holders who use their ATM's. It was the first time (October 3, 1999) in the U.S. that voters had the opportunity to act on the issue.

The Guardian, the first self-contained home refrigerator and the predecessor of Frigidaire units, was developed in 1915.

As stoves moved into the kitchen, they became specialized cooking appliances. Ranges burning wood or coal were replaced by gas and electric stoves. Raytheon unveiled the first microwave oven in 1947.

French, those fussy purveyors of gourmet fare (no McDonalds or KFC), gave the first thumbs up to preserved food.

Sony's Cyber-Shot DSC-F505 is the world's first digital camera to sport a 5x optical zoom lens.

The first modern hot water heating system was installed in a French castle in 1777. In 1784, James Watt used steam pipes to heat his office—the first use of steam heat.

Redlines revolution is the first snowmobile with a four-stroke engine. It produces 95 percent (95%) fewer hydrocarbons and delivers better fuel economy than a same size two-stroke.

With the first keyboard light, IBM's I Series laptop shines the way—literally—for typists in darkened airplane cabins.

If your ice cream has ever tasted like pastrami on rye, you understand the problem of circulating refrigerator odors. Samsung's Twin Cooling refrigerators have a single solution—the first totally separate cooling systems for the fridge and the freezer.

Endless summer and perpetual winter, simultaneously? Gotcha Glacier, the first indoor snowboard and Surf Park in the U.S., boasts perfect powder snow and killer waves no matter what the calendar says.

Wolcraft's Quick-Jaw bar clamps are the first with bidirectional one-hand control. Pull the lever to tighten the clamp, and the back lever.

The first phone to work in the U.S. (1,900 MHz) and two world wide GSM frequencies (1,800-and 900 MHz), Motorola's Timeport Triband mobile phone works in more than 120 countries. The 3.8 ounce phone supports voice dialing, voice memo, fax and five-line graphical display.

Wasbash, a small, liberal arts college in Crawfordsville, Indiana, is all male—one of ONLY three such schools in the U.S.

(President Clinton impeachment attorney, David Kendall, was a Wabash alumnus). Wabash was the first college to produce the Pulitzer—prizewinning play about AIDS, Angels in America.

When you buy potato salad, or any other deli item, ONLY the food must be charged for when weighed.

Chicago inventor Whitcomb Judson designed a "clasp locker" that today is recognized as the first zipper.

Never mind that Appleseed—real name: John Chapman—ONLY lived in Leominster, Massachusetts until he was 6.

Australia officially recognizes the Aborigines in 1999 as the nations first people and praised them for their deep kinship with their lands and for the ancient and continuing cultures.

The Rev. William Richard Tolbert of Liberia ancestors were among the first black American settlers, who started arriving on the lush Atlantic coast in 1821. More than 12,000 others followed.

On November 7, 1999 the world's longest ruling political party (Institutional Revolutionary Party—PRI—in Mexico) held it's first ever U.S.—style primary to select its presidential candidate.

Steven Weinberg, who won the 1979 Nobel Prize in physics, was named the first recipient of the "Emperor Has No Clothes Award" by the Freedom from Religion Foundation, which honors public figures who speak out about the non religious views.

In search of better spare parts, scientists for the first time have grown heart valves from scratch in a test tube, and then shown that they work like natures' own—at least in animals.

Joseph Chebet of Kenya won both the Boston and New York marathons in 1999, making him just the third runner to complete a Boston—New York sweep in the one year and the first non-American to achieve that feat (Bill Rogers, 1978-79; Alberto Salazar, 1981 are the ONLY other two).

Scientists in various countries—including Japan—have been cloning livestock since the birth in 1996 of the sheep Dolly, the first animal to be cloned from an adult mammal.

English monk Roger Bacon made the first recorded observations about the use of lenses for vision correction.

The first batteries for consumer use appeared in the late 19th century. Within a few decades, carbon-zinc dry cells made it possible to produce small, battery-powered devices like radios and flashlights.

Warren Morrison of Bell Telephone Laboratories used vibrating quartz crystal to devise a clock that was far more accurate than any mechanical timepiece. A miniature version of Morrison's vibrating crystal made it possible to create the first quartz wristwatch in 1967.

An American leather tanner named John Loud invented the first pen to apply it with a rolling ball; he used it for many hides. Some 14 million are sold daily.

An electronic paper from E Ink, used for the first time in 1999 for several J.C. Penny store signs, offers the look and feel of the real thing without any need to recycle.

Venison—the staple of America's first hunters.

Richard Nixon's Watergate-era lawyer spoke publicly for the first time (November 13, 1999) about events following the president's resignation in 1974, saying, Nixon initially opposed Gerald Ford's "full, free, and absolute" pardon (September 8, 1974) Nixon died in April 1994.

On November 15, 1999 France's announcement by Justice Minister Elisabeth Guigou comes on the heels of a dramatic declaration that Jewish children orphaned during the Holocaust will for the first time receive monetary compensation for their suffering.

Oxidation has been suspected in aging since 1956, when it was first proposed that free radicals—unstable molecules with an unpaired electron—attack cells.

The first Hooters Opened in Clearwater, Florida in 1983.

For the first time, bonuses of $6,000 were offered for two-year enlistment in some jobs in the U.S. Army starting in November 1999. Until then, cash bonuses were given ONLY for three-year or longer terms of service.

British Prime Minister Tony Blair and his wife (45 years old) Cherie Booth, had their fourth child in May 2000. This is the first time since 1848 that a sitting PM of Britain had a child while in office.

Using gasoline and liquid oxygen, Robert Goddard launched the world's first liquid propellant rocket in 1926 from his Aunt Effie's farm in Auburn, Massachusetts.

William Shakespeare was the greatest Briton of all time and Margaret Thatcher, the Conservative Prime Minister from 1979 to 1990, was the ONLY living listed in the top 50 (she wad ranked 39th) list of greatest Britons of all times.

The Soviet Union lofted Sputnik 1, the world's first artificial satellite on October 4, 1957, and in doing so opened the Space Age.

Toyota was first with a gasoline-electric hybrid, the Prius. Hybrids use both electric and combustion engines to achieve low emissions and high fuel economy.

Platelets help with clotting and are especially important for children undergoing chemotherapy and organ transplant.

Because they can ONLY be stored for five days, a constant supply is needed.

In the first half of the 20th century, most companies were run by founders who owned the bulk of their companies stock.

China is one step closer to catching up to the U.S. and Russia Space Programs after coordinating it's first unmanned test (November '99) of a spacecraft designed to carry astronauts.

1999 was the first year that more rhinos in Africa were darted for sport than were killed by hunters.

In 1950 Jerrold Electronics wired the first cable television system in the eastern United States in Lansford and Mahanoy, Pennsylvania.

In November 1900, 31 automakers displayed cars at the first National Auto Show.

On January 2, 1921 the first radio broadcast of religious services was aired on KDKA, Pittsburg, Pennsylvania.

NASA selected its first women astronauts in January 1978.

Leonard Thompson, age 14, January 23, 1922 became the first diabetic to receive insulin injections in Toronto, Canada.

The first car insurance issued in the U.S. was February 1, 1898.

NBC broadcast the first daily newsreel in February 1948.

First U.S. credit union was opened in Manchester, New Hampshire April, 1909.

In May 1933 Nellie Taylor Ross became the first women director of a U.S. Mint.

The first recorded U.S. earthquake, June 1638, Plymouth, Massachusetts.

The first prime time TV big-money show, "The $64,000 Question", premiered on June 6, 1955.

The first female students were admitted to U.S. Naval Academy at Annapolis, Maryland on July 6, 1976.

The first televised speech form the White House—October 5, 1947.

On October 22, 1956 the first gorilla was born in captivity.

On July 28, 1933 the first singing telegram was delivered.

In the first known case of its kind (October 2000), a Colorado couple created a test-tube baby who was genetically screened and selected in the hope he could save the life of his 6 year old sister.

Tim McGraw and Faith Hill became the first husband and wife to win best male and female vocalist awards in the same year (2000) at the Country Music Association Awards.

Davo Karnicar of Slovenia, a 38 year old (October 2000) ski instructor became the first person to descent Mt. Everest uninterrupted from the 29,035 foot summit to the base camp at 17,472 feet on skis, a trip that took five hours.

RCA's REB1100 eBook is the first paperback-size electronic book with a built-modem.

VIBRAM'S VERTIGE SOLE is the first outer sole to be designed with a climbing crampon in mind.

Angela Perez Baraquio became the first Miss America of Asian-American descent (October 2000).

Teen magazine became the first magazine to do business with Ultigo, a company whose technology allows reorders to interact online with firms whose products appear in print.

The mango was carried to the West Indies—first to Barbados about 1742 and later to the Dominican Republic.

One of the first things to go seems to be real estate after a celebrity breakup.

Robert B. Thomas published the first edition of the Old Farmer's Almanac in 1792.

The FDA in the year 2000 approved the first vaccine, LYMErix, against the tick-borne illness.

The first medical school for women opened in Boston in November 1848.

The first life insurance policy issued to a woman on November 9, 1850.

The first Army-Navy football game, November 29, 1890 (Navy 24—Army 0).

Ladies' Home Journal first issue was published December 6, 1883.

Colour TV sets were first put on sale on December 30, 1953.

Canned beer was sold for the first time on January 24, 1935 in Richmond, Virginia.

McDonald's opened its first restaurant in the Soviet Union on December 31, 1990.

Elm Farm Ollie became the first dairy cow to fly in an airplane on February 28, 1930.

The first People magazine issue was on March 5, 1974.

The first Japanese cherry trees were planted along the Potomac River in 1912.

The first airline flight attendant was Ellen Church on May 15, 1930.

The first U.S. daily newspaper was published on May 30, 1783.

The first minimum wage in the U.S. was established at $.40 per hour on July 12, 1933.

The gas chamber was first used in 1924 to execute convicted criminals.

On December 7, 1982, Charlie Brooks was the first person to be executed by lethal injection.

Glenfiddich is the ONLY Highland Scotch whisky to use a single source of natural spring water through every phase of the distillation, maturation and bottling.

There are ONLY 6,000 families in the world that control all the wealth, Bill Gates, CEO of Microsoft is not one of them.

ONLY 1 percent to 2 percent of the millions of kids who join Boy Scouts make it to Eagle Scout.

The first AOL/Take Action Innovator Award went to Megan Corley of Anacortes, Washington on March 30, 2000 in New York City.

The first time (4/7/00) in its 85 year history, tiny Graham Hill high school in Weleetka, Oklahoma dressed itself for a dance and having their first prom.

Built between 1650 and 1680, the Revere House is the oldest dwelling in Boston. It is the ONLY colonial building of this type to survive in the heart of any American City.

Japans first arrest on April 7, 2000 under newly introduced anti-stalking ordinances.

The new state of Israel wanted Albert Einstein to be their first Prime Minister. He left all his works to the Hebrew University and his violin to his grandson.

Speaker Dennis Hastert appointed a Chicago priest, the Reverend Daniel P. Coughlin, as House Chaplain March 23, 2000, Coughlin became the first Roman Catholic to hold the position ministering to lawmakers and their families.

ABC TV President Patricia Fili-Krushel, the first female of major television network.

The first Nuclear Security Decision makers Forum was held in March 2000 in Albuquerque, New Mexico, which attracted nearly 200 of the U.S. top nuclear scientists, engineers and administrators.

Lt. Gen. Claudia Kennedy is the first female three-star general in the history of the U.S. Army.

Senator John McCain was the first person to use state of the art confetti at his victory speech in his run for the U.S. presidency in 2000.

The USS Holland was the first submarine acquired by the U.S. Navy in 1900.

With electronic equipment becoming obsolete at an increasingly rapid rate, Massachusetts is instituting the U.S. first ban (4/1/00) on disposal of computer screens, TV sets and other glass picture tubes in landfills in incinerators.

In March 2000 Erin Nicole Claunch became the first female in school history of Virginia Military Institute (VMI) to be named battalion commander.

Atomic clocks keep time by precisely counting the vibrations of atoms. The first version was invented in 1949 with the help of physicists who worked on the Manhattan Project.

For the first time in the history of the U.S. breakfast-cereal industry, Kellogg Company isn't king. General Mills Inc. surpassed Kellogg in November '99 to become the top cereal maker in terms of volume, reinforcing it's already No. 1 status in terms of dollars.

ON October 18, 1907 the first Wireless Press Message across the Atlantic.

On February 23, 1997 scientists report the first cloning ever of an adult mammal.

Conservatives win British vote Margaret "Iron Lady" Thatcher became the first woman to head a European government May 4, 1979.

The Nobel Peace Prize (Dr. Alfred B. Nobel, the Swedish inventor of dynamite) has taken on a broader interpretation of "peace" since the first one was awarded in 1901.

Scientists applauded English churchmen nodded a qualified approval and the British press turned somersaults today (July 26, 1978) to welcome the world's first baby (5-pound-12 ounce girl) born from an egg fertilized in a laboratory.

Anthony Fiala, a turn-of-the-century explorer, signed on as a photographer in 1901 expedition to the North Pole. He made the first moving pictures ever taken in the Arctic.

On May 29, 1953 a lanky New Zealand beekeeper, Edmond Hillary became the first to set foot atop *Mount Everest. His companion Tenzing Norgay, a Buddhist Sherpa was the only one photographed at the summit. *(Mount Everest for whom the height was named in 1852 belongs to Sir George Everest, Surveyor General of India.)

James McDermott, who earned $4 million in 1998 as head of Keefe Bruyette & Woods, is the first CEO ever to be charged by the SEC for insider trading.

In 1995, biologist J. Craig Venter, then head of the Institute for Genomic Research in Rockville, Md., published the entire DNA sequence of the microbe Haemophilus influenza—the first sequence of a free-living organism.

In 1910, at the Pennsylvania Railroad depot in Terre Haute, Ind., the first pay toilet was installed.

Joseph Engelberger, sold General Motors its first industrial robot for assembly-line work in 1961.

Israel released 26 prisoners on Dec. 29, 1999, it was the first time Israel freed Palestinians who had killed Israeli's or terrorists as part of a negotiated peace process release.

The first section of the unique 116-year-old full Oxford English Dictionary, edited by Sir James Murray, came out in 1884 and the first edition in 1928.

Michael Jordon is the only person (as of 1999) to win AP Athlete of the Year three times.

In 1935 the first sulfa drug, an antibiotic, was discovered.

Consulting editor Wernher von Braun previewed the first U.S.—U.S.S.R. space rendezvous in July 1974—the Apollo—Soyuz linkup.

Harvard University became the first to bar its faculty from consulting, advising, or joining the board of student-run business.

Archie Griffin is the ONLY two-time recipient of the Heisman Trophy, earned the award in 1974 and '75 as a shifty 5'9", 180 pound dervish with a unique ability to pinball off tacklers and then jet down the field. In 1973 Griffin became the first sophomore to earn Big Ten MVP honours, setting the conference single-season rushing record with 1,577 yards.

Teddy Roosevelt in 1905 was the ONLY U.S. President to be awarded the Nobel Peace Prize.

Jesse Gelsinger of Tucson, Arizona with a rare liver disorder whose death in September '99 became the first ever linked to gene therapy.

A restaurant "Starcatcher" in English in this Taipei, Taiwan, suburb is believed to be the ONLY eatery in the world built above the flue of a garbage incinerator.

Louisiana opened the first juvenile boot camp in 1985.

The Susan B. Anthony dollar (1979-81) paid tribute to the tireless crusader for Women's Rights, and was the first circulating U.S. coin to depict an actual woman (rather than a mythical figure).

New Hampshire is the first state to restrict lead tackle.

Maurice Richard (the Rocket), the first NHL player to score 50 goals in 50 games (1944-45).

Steffi Graf is the ONLY pro tennis player to win all four Grand Slam events at least four times.

Rod Laver, the left-handed Aussie is the ONLY player to win two Grand Slams (1962, '69); in all, the Rocket won 11 Grand Slam singles titles.

Al Oerter, the four-time Olympic discus champion is one of ONLY two athletes to win gold in four consecutive Games ('56, '60, '64, and '68).

Shedding a little more public light on the monarch at work, Buckingham Palace released Dec. 2, 1999 the first footage of Queen Elizabeth granting honors and awards at a royal investiture.

By marrying King Albert II's son (Prince Philippe of Belgium) Princess Mathilde is set to become Belgium's first homegrown queen in the country's 169-year history.

Terence Young, the first James Bond "007" director, once remarked that, with the exception of Lassie, Sean Connery was the ONLY star he knew who had never been spoiled by success.

ONLY the female mosquito need blood meals to provide protein for development of their eggs.

Green Bank, West Virginia, home of the National Radio Astronomy Observatory is the world's ONLY Quiet Zone. The Quiet Zone ONLY provides protection form ground-based transmitters.

The Japanese vine Kudzu, also called "the vine that ate the South" was first introduced as an ornamental at Philadelphia's 1876 Centennial Exposition.

Medical imaging has evolved dramatically since 1985 when physicist William Konrad Rontgen made his wife's hand the subject of the first x-ray photograph.

Seventy million people watched the debate between Richard Nixon and John F. Kennedy (Kennedy won), the first covered by all three major networks. It was September 26, 1960.

In 1944 ONLY Oklahoma, New Mexico and Louisiana still allows the poultry practice of cockfighting legal.

Leaders of an Indian Tribe (Pyramid Lake Paiute) entered a first-of-its-kind agreement with the U.S. government November 29, 1999 in which they assume significant control of water resources off their reservation in an effort to save endangered fish—cui ui (pronounced "Kee-wee").

Kuwait boasts the ONLY legislature in the Arab Gulf; its 37-year-old democracy is known as that of the "chosen few" because it represents less than 14 percent (14%) of Kuwaitis.

A will allows you to arrange ONLY for the future transfer of assets to your heirs. It does not assure you how well these assets will be managed, nor will it help your children avoid paying unnecessary estate taxes when your surviving spouse dies.

One million Italian lira is ONLY $550 U.S. dollars—1999 rate.

Denver schools recently became the first in the U.

S. to approve a plan tying teacher salaries to student performance. (1999)

Despite a diplomatic dispute between the United States and Cuba, regular, direct passenger-flights from new York to Havana are resuming for the first time (December 3, 1999) in nearly four decades.

Having braved hurricanes and bouts of despair, a wobbly-kneed but triumphant Kentucky lawyer paddled to the French Caribbean island of Guadeloupe on December 3, 1999 and became the first American—and the first woman—to row across the Atlantic alone.

Paul McCartney plans a solo concert December 14, 1999 at the Cavern Club, a rebuilt version of the Liverpool venue where the Beatles performed for the first time in 1961. McCartney first appeared with the Quarrymen in 1958.

In 1890, while en route to the U.S. Military Academy for the first Army-Navy game, the midshipmen stole a goat to serve as their mascot.

In 1959 the S.S. Savannah became the first nuclear-powered merchant ship, is launched at New York Shipbuilding in Camden, N.J.

In 1849 a group of Quaker businessmen, clergy and physicians led by William J. Mullen founded the Female Medical College of Pennsylvania, the world's first medical school for women.

General Eric Shinseki, Chief of the U.S. Army, a Japanese-American wounded Viet Nam veteran, the first nonwhite to hold the Army's top command post.

Harvard educated Dr. Alan Keyes, presidential hopeful for the year 2000, was the first African-American to win the American Legion National Oratorical Championship at 16 in 1967, and the youngest winner up to that time.

Joseph Horn and Frank Hardart opened the U.S. first Automat at 818 Chestnut, Philadelphia, Pa in 1902, serving the first drip-filtered coffee in town.

Kodak and Sanyo have teamed up to create the first full-colour organic electroluminescent display. The thin-as-a-dime technology demonstrator consists of layers of carbon-based compounds that emit light when current is applied.

Researchers at Organogenesis have developed the first artificial vein that interacts with the body like a real healthy blood vessel.

The first mannequin with the size and physiology of a child, it can be programmed to display life-threatening symptoms commonly seen in hospital emergency rooms, including allergic reactions, adverse drug responses and heart problems.

The Sierra Club, one of the U.S. premier environmental groups and a harsh critic of automobile industry, broke a 108 year tradition of refusing to lend its name to commercial products. It issued an endorsement—its first ever—for a car, the Honda Insight, a 70-mile-per-gallon, gas-electric hybrid coupe.

Jemima Vernette Blaise, 6 lbs. 11 oz., born in Jackson Memorial Hospital, Miami, Florida became the first baby of the millennium.

Ann Miller was the first person saved by penicillin at age 57. She died in 1999.

The United States is the ONLY nation in the world since 1997 known to have executed inmates who committed crimes while under the age of 18. The first known execution of a teen-ager took place in 1642, in Plymouth Colony, Massachusetts.

Ray York, who rode Determine to victory in the 1954 Kentucky Derby, is set to become the first jockey to compete in seven different decades when he rides Cerebra on January 13, 2000 eighth race at Santa Anita.

The first flight of an aircraft powered by jet engine occurred in 1939 in Germany.

President Franklin D. Roosevelt made the First Inaugural Address on March 4, 1933 in Washington, D.C.

For the first time since AIDS captured the nation's attention in the early 1980's more Black and Hispanic gay men were diagnosed with the disease than White gay men in 1998.

The largest U.S gun manufacturer (Sturm, Ruger & Co.) is instructing distributors not to sell its firearms at gun shows, apparently the first of its kind.

Each fall, the bright orange-and-black monarch butterfly, by the millions flies thousands of miles from breeding grounds in North America to winter long grounds in New Mexico—the ONLY insect known to migrate such a long distance.

After traveling 4,000 miles a minuteman was intercepted 140 miles above the Pacific in the first successful test of an exo-atmospheric kill vehicle (EKV).

The first party in Times Square was on December 31, 1904, the original New Year's Ball, which had its debut drop in 1907, had just 100 light bulbs.

In 27 B.C. Augustus becomes first Roman emperor.

Peter was Jesus' favoured disciple and leader of the first Christian community.

In 1978, the year of three popes, the Polish Cardinal Karol Wojtyla becomes John Paul II, the first non-Italian leader of the Roman Church in 455 years.

Activist Margaret Sanger, her sister, Ethel Bryne, and an associate, Fania Mindell, were arrested (distributing contraceptives under NY State's anti-obscenity statutes was considered obscene) for opening the first birth control clinic in America in Brooklyn on October 16, 1916.

Drivers crossing into Mexico had to leave deposits of up to $800 beginning December 1, 1999, the first day of an unpopular Mexican program aimed at preventing the illegal importation of cars registered in the United States.

Virtual tourists visiting NASA's Web site will find pictures, weather reports, science data and the first sound clips ever beamed to Earth from 157 million miles away.

It is not until 1528 that the first chocolate recipe reaches Europe with Hernando Cortez, who returns home with a ship full of cocoa beans, mixes up some hot chocolate, and serves it to the Holy Roman Emperor Charles V.

In 1824 Mrs. Randolph published Virginia Housewife, the first truly American cookbook and probably the greatest.

Wo Kee in 1878 started the first Chinese grocery store in New York City, opens on Mott Street.

The Jupiter—Tequesta Athletic Association which serves 6,000 children 5 to 18 years old, is the first in the U.S. to make sportsmanship training for parents a prerequisite.

An instrument called Light Detection and Ranging will be Russia's first instrument aboard a NASA planetary Lander—Mars Polar Lander.

In 1996 General Instrument Corp. (GI) introduces the first digital cable system.

To make the first underwater colour photographs ever published, Charles Martin and W.H. Longley set off huge charges of flash powder at the surface January 1927.

Scientist first identifies HIV, the virus that causes AIDS, in 1983.

In 1936 Irvine and Merriel Gardner traveled across Russia with a 14-foot-long telescope to make the first colour photograph of a solar eclipse in February 1937.

The first thing people usually ask each other when they meet is "What's your name" and the second is "What do you do".

New York City was the site of the first Jimmy Carter Work Project (JCWP)—a one week work contribution by Jimmy and Rosalynn Carter—part of the Habitat for Humanity International.

Quantum theory (holds that energy, light and matter sometimes behave more like particles than waves) was developed and elaborated on in the first third of the 20th century by such figures as Max Planck, Albert Einstein, Niels Bohr and Werner Heisenberg.

Casey Martin rides his golf cart in his debut 1/19/2000 as the first PGA Tour member on wheels. Martin suffers from a circulatory disease in his right leg that makes it virtually impossible for him to walk 18 holes over four rounds.

Professional rodeo is the ONLY major competitive sport that evolved form an actual working lifestyle.

Hosea Williams of the Southern Christian led 600 people on March 7, 1965, in a first- and failed-attempt to march on Montgomery. On that Bloody Sunday state troopers and sheriffs' deputies wielded clubs and tear gas.

The march from Selma to Montgomery is the first national historic trail where many of the marchers were still alive in the year 2000.

Stanton Katchatag, an 82-year-old Inupiaq Eskimo from Alaska, who lives in an isolated wind swept village near the frozen Bering Sea, became the first American to participate in U.S. Census 2000.

Senator Jesse Helms, the Senate Foreign Relations Committee Chairman, became the first-ever U.S. lawmaker to address the U.N. Security Council on January 20, 2000.

Haitians made their biggest political gain in December 1999 when residents of El Portal, a small village that borders Miami, elected three Haitians to its five-member council. It is the first municipality in the U.S. to have a Haitian majority.

World Wrestling Federation Entertainment (WWF) on January 14, 2000 defeated a "cyber-squatter" who registered an Internet domain name using the company's trademark. It was the first such case resolved through the Internet's oversight board.

A 62 year blind man can read large letters and navigate around big objects by using a tiny camera wired directly to his brain, the first artificial eye to provide useful vision.

The Experian qualifications database (UK)—the first of its kind anywhere in the world—will carry all of the qualifications logged with the Higher Educations Statistics Agency (HESA) since 1995, including degrees in medicine and law.

Jim Bakker and his first wife Tammy, were the first couple of televised religion until he was convicted in 1989 of defrauding followers of $158 million.

HUD is targeting Ryan Wilson of Fishtown violated the Fair Housing Act by threatening Bonnie Jouhari on Web sites. These charges are believed to be the first by a federal agency against a known hate Web site.

April Heinrich officially was named head coach 1/18/2000, becoming the first woman to head the Women's' Soccer Team and replacing Tony DiCicco who guided the Americans to the World Cup title last summer before resigning in November '99.

Johannes Keplers first two laws of planetary motion were published in 1609 (the third appeared in 1619).

The world's first official observatory was established in Leiden in the Netherlands in 1632.

In 1962 the first x-ray source was discovered in Scorpius.

The first quasar was discovered in 1963.

The first pulsar was discovered by Jocelyn Bell and Antony Hewish in 1967.

The first crewed (Neil Armstrong and Edwin Aldrin) moon landing was made by U.S. Astronauts in July 1969.

On February 3, 1990 Magellon arrived at Venus and transmitted its first pictures August 16, 1990.

In 1942 the first controlled nuclear chain reaction is achieved by Enrico Fermi.

The first high temperature superconductor was discovered in 1986, able to conduct electricity without resistance at a temperature of—238°C—396°F.

Leo Szilard, a Hungarian—born U.S. physicist who died in 1995 linked up with Sir John Cockcraft to produce the first disintegration of a nucleus in the first successful use of a particle accelerator.

Franz Wohler converts ammonium cyanate into urea—the first synthesis of an organic compound from an inorganic substance in 1828.

John Newlands devised the first periodic table of the elements in 1864.

William Ramsey and Lord Rayleigh discover the first inert gasses, argon, in 1894.

John Wesley who died in 1920 was a U.S. inventor who produced the first artificial plastic.

English chemist, William Perkin, who lived from 1838-1907, first extracted dye mauve, and founded the modern dye industry.

In 1862 Hemoglobin is first crystallized.

In 1921 Insulin is first isolated from the pancreas by Frederick Banting and Charles Best.

In 1927 thyroxine is first synthesized.

In 1943 the role of DNA in genetic inheritance is first demonstrated by Oswald Avery, Colin MacLead and Maclyn McCarty.

Insulin is first synthesized in 1965.

Human insulin is first produced by genetic engineering in 1978.

U.S. geneticists construct the first human chromosome in 1997.

Jean-Pierre Blanchard and John J. Joffries make the first balloon crossing of the English Channel in 1785.

George Cayley flies the first true airplane, a model glider 5 feet long.

Truth is the first casualty in war.

In 1903 the first powered and controlled flight of a heavier-than-air craft (airplane) by Orville Wright, at Kitty Hawk, North Carolina, U.S.

In 1927 Charles Lindbergh makes the first west-east solo nonstop flight across the Atlantic.

In 1928 the first transpacific flight from San Francisco to Brisbane by Charles Lindbergh and C.T. Ulm.

In 1930 Frank Whittle patents the jet engine; Amy Johnson becomes the first woman to fly solo from England to Australia.

The first fully pressurized aircraft, the Lockheed XC-35, comes into service in 1937.

The first person to fly the Heinkel jet plane was Erich Warsitz in Germany and the first to design a helicopter with a large main rotor and a smaller tail rotor was Igor Sikorsky in 1939.

The first aircraft to fly faster than the speed of sound was a rocket-powered plane, the Bell X-1

The first vertical takeoff aircraft (VTOL), the Rolls-Royce "Flying Bedstead" was tested in 1953.

In 1968 the world's first supersonic airliner, the Russian TU-144, flies for the first time.

In 1978 a U.S. team makes the first transatlantic crossing by balloon, in the helium filled Double Eagle II.

In 1987 Richard Branson and Per Lindstrand make the first transatlantic crossing by a hot-air balloon, the Virgin Atlantic Challenger.

In 1994 the Boeing 777 airliner makes its first flight.

In 1922 Insulin was first used to treat diabetes.

In 1967 Dr. Christiaan Barnard, a South African, performs the first human heart-transplant operation.

In 1972 the CAT Scan, pioneered by Godfrey Hounsfield, is first used to image the human brain.

In the 1980's AIDS (acquired immuno-deficiency syndrome) is first recognized in the U.S., Barbara McClintock's discovery of the transposable gene is recognized.

The first vaccine against leprosy is developed in 1984.

The first trials of gene therapy against cystic fibrosis takes place in the United States in 1993.

The first person to end his life by legally sanctioned euthanasia was an Australian man, Ben Dent in 1996.

James Black, a Scottish born pharmacologist who developed the first beta-blocker drugs as well as anti-ulcer drugs.

Elizabeth Anderson who died in 1917 was an English physician, and the first English woman to qualify in medicine.

Elizabeth Blackwell (1821-1910) was an English-born U.S. physician who was the first woman to qualify in medicine in the United States.

Alexander Fleming, Scottish bacteriologist who discovered the first antibiotic drug, penicillin.

Shibasaburo Kitasato who died in 1931 was a Japanese bacteriologist who discovered the plague bacillus and was the first to grow the tetanus bacillus in pure culture.

The workable steam-powered engine is developed by Thomas Newcomen in 1712.

The first Canal Act is passed by the British Parliament; this leads to the construction of a national network of inland waterways for transportation and industrial supplies in 1759.

The first true industrial lathe is invented, virtually simultaneously, by Henry Maudslay in England and David Wilkinson the United States.

In 1802 the first electric Battery capable of mass production is designed by William Cruickshank in England.

In 1825 the first regular railroad services start between Stockton and Darlington in northeast England.

In 1833 the first effective Factory Act is passed in Britain regulating child labour in cotton mills.

Jan Tinbergen born in 1903, a Dutch economist, who helped developed the field of econometrics and shared the first Nobel Prize for Economics.

Alex Charles Tocqueville, a French political and social theorist who authored the first analytical study of U.S. society: De la Democratie en Amerique/Democracy in America.

The U.S. Air Force first jet bombers were the B-47's.

The first mass-produced calculator, the Arithometer, is developed by Charles Thomas de Colmar in 1820.

The first program-controlled calculator, the Harvard University Mark 1 or Automatic Sequence Controlled Calculator, was introduced in 1943.

The first commercially produced computer came out by Launch of Ferranti Mark in 1951.

The first integrated circuit is constructed in 1958.

In 1965 the first supercomputer, the Control Data CD6600, is developed.

In 1971 the first microprocessor, the Intel 4004, was introduced.

In 1974 Clip-4, the first computer with a parallel architecture is developed by John Backus at IBM.

In 1975 Altair 8800, the first personal computer (PC) or microcomputer, is launched.

The first "off-the-shelf," the Inmos T414 transputer, microprocessor for building parallel computers, is announced in 1985.

The first optical microprocessor, which uses light instead of electricity, is developed in 1988.

The first time a computer has beaten a human grand master IBM's Deep Blue beats grand master Gary Kosporov at chess in 1996.

The first account of the human body was given by Andreas Vesalius in 1543.

In 1900 Karl Landsteiner identifies the first three blood groups, later designated A, B and O.

The first Mercedes takes to the roads; it is the direct ancestor of the present car—came on the line in 1901.

The first rotary gasoline was built by Felix Wankel in 1957.

The first mass-produced car with four-wheel steering, the Mitsubishi Galant, is launched in 1989.

In 1996 Daimler-Benz unveils the first fuel-cell-powered car.

Marc Andreessen, born in 1972, a U.S. systems developer and co-author of the first widely available graphical browser for the World Wide Web.

Seymour Roger Cray who died in 1996, a U.S. computer scientist and pioneer in the field of supercomputing. In 1972 he formed Cray Research to build the first popular supercomputer; the Cray-1, released in 1976.

Herman Hollerith (1860-1929) U.S. inventor of a mechanical tabulating machine, the first device for high-volume data processing.

John William who lived from 1907 to 1980 was a U.S. physicist and engineer who, in 1946, constructed the first general purpose computer.

Clive Sinclair who was born in 1940 is a British electronics engineer. He produced the first widely available pocket calculator, pocket and wristwatch televisions and a series of home computers.

The United States is the ONLY industrialized nation in the world that permits prescription drugs to be advertised directly to consumers on TV and in print.

Richard Paez is the first Mexican-American to serve as a federal judge in Los Angeles; he was nominated in January 1996 to a higher judgeship on the Ninth Circuit Court of Appeals.

At the beginning of the year 2000 Mazda is the ONLY major automaker with a rotary engine in volume production.

In January 2000 the Thomas Jefferson Memorial Foundation acknowledged for the first time that Jefferson is likely father of one, if not all six, of slave Sally Hemings' children.

RCD—rabid calicivirus disease (the scientific name is rabbit hemorrhagic disease) was first reported in China in 1984, and the international trade in domestic rabbits aided its spread.

In the year 2000 ONLY 2.1 percent (2.1%) of all the cars and light trucks on the road are powered by diesels, and most of those are medium or heavy-duty pickups used for serious hauling.

With near flawless precision, a spacecraft (Near Earth Asteroid Rendezvous)—NEAR—slipped into orbit 1/14/2000 around the asteroid Eros, becoming the first manmade satellite of an asteroid.

Last fall (1999) thousands of cancer patients tried to enroll in the first human trials of Endostatin protein, an experimental drug shown to shrink tumors in mice.

On a cold blustery day in November 1919, 684 official delegates and 234 non-voting leaders gathered in Minneapolis for the first National Convention of the American Legion.

Bishop Bevilacqua's installation as the first Italian-American archbishop of Philadelphia took place February 27, 1987, 27 years to the day after Cardinal Krol's appointment.

On Wednesday February 2, 2000 is the first time in the new millennium that all the date (2/2/2000) is even numbers.

Alfred Hitchcock's first movie in colour was Rope.

The Cadillac Northstar LMP sports car makes its debut at Daytona International February 3, 2000 for the first time since 1950.

Launched in 1967 the Queen Elizabeth II Cruise ship is the ONLY one making the transatlantic crossing.

Britain's Conservative Party novelist, Jeffrey Archer is London's first elected lord mayor.

The first Congressional Gold Medal of Honour—the U.S. highest civilian award—was given to George Washington.

The ONLY two governors to become U.S. president west of the Mississippi were Ronald Reagan and William "Bill" Clinton.

By all accounts Fusac Ofa's election as Japan's first governor was a major victory for women in a political world that remains the realm of men.

Koshmir is the ONLY predominantly Muslim region in mostly Hindu India and has been the center of a 10-year insurgency (as of 2000) by several militant groups fighting for independence or union with Pakistan.

For the first time, May 11, 2000, the three Tenors—Jose Carreras, Placido Domingo and Luciana Pavarotti—will all appeared at the Metropolitan Opera on the same night.

The first German words ever spoken in Israel's' parliament were a plea on February 16. 2000 by German President Johannes Rav for forgiveness for the Holocaust.

The oldest manually operated church bells in the U.S. are in the Church of the Holy Trinity on Rittenhouse, Philadelphia, PA. They were first rung at the opening session of the General Convention of the Protestant Episcopal Church on October 3, 1883.

Nine spectators and 11 drivers were injured on February 18, 2000 in a fiery crash of 13 pickup trucks competing in the debut (first) of the NASCAR Craftsman Truck series at the Daytona International Speedway.

In 1998 Jennifer Dunn became the first woman to run for U.S. House of Representative House Majority Leader.

Pidyon haben (the ancient Jewish ceremony that symbolically "redeems a firstborn son") occurs ONLY when a couple's first child is naturally born and male and when neither parent is the child of a male kohen or levite.

George Washington is the ONLY president who never lived in the White House. Washington lived in New York City and Philadelphia during his presidency.

President Hosni Mubarak became the first Egyptian leader to visit (2/19/2000) the Lebanese capitol since Lebanon won independence in 1943.

President Dwight Eisenhower held the first televised press conference in 1955.

ONLY 10 heart-lung-liver transplants have been performed worldwide, all on adults as of February 2000.

In a wolf pack, Alfa males eat first—always.

"Sesame Street" first broadcast in 1969 is seen in 140 countries.

A Florida processor Colorado Boxed Beef Company is expected to be the first to test the market (2/22/2000) that allows the irradiation of raw beef, pork and lamb. To its advocates, irradiation could be one of the biggest advancements in food safety since pasteurization of milk.

The United States' first combined primary and secondary public school (The Smith School) for Blacks has been reopened (2/22/2000) as a monument to Boston's often turbulent history of race in schools.

Arizona's Todd Stottlemyre and his father Mel are the ONLY father-and-son duo with 100 or more major league victories apiece.

Belize is the ONLY country in Central America that sings their national anthem in English.

In 1891, Luther Cary became the first person to be officially recognized as the fastest man on earth.

Viktor I. Patsayer was the first person to celebrate a birthday in space—age 38 on June 19, 1971.

Megapodes are the ONLY birds in the world that don't sit on their eggs to incubate them. Inhabiting volcanic Pacific Islands, these fowl-like birds, related to partridges, bury their eggs.

Richard Ford's sixth novel, Independence Day, set during the 4th of July weekend, is the first novel to win both the Pulitzer Prize and PEN/Faulkner Award for fiction.

Perry Como sold the first million selling U.S. singles with Catch a Falling Star in 1958.

Bill Haley and His Comets was the first American group to have a No.1 single in the UK—Rock Around the Clock in 1955.

The Tornados was the first British group to have a No. 1 single in the U.S.—Telstar in 1962.

Al Martino was the first American solo artist to have a No.1 single in the UK—Here in my Heart in 1952.

Candy manufacturer Franklin C. Mars established his first business in Tacoma, Washington, in 1911 and formed the Mar-O-Bar company in Minneapolis (later moving it to Chicago) in 1922, with the first of its products, the Milky Way Bar.

Pope John Paul II begins his millennium pilgrimages to biblical sites with a visit to Egypt on February 24, 2000. The three-day-trip—the first by a Roman Catholic pontiff to Egypt.

The first video every played on MTV was Buggles' "Video Killed the Radio Star".

The first permanent settlement in what is now U.S. territory was St. Augustine, Fla., founded in 1565 by Spaniard Pedro Menendez de Aviles.

In the first experiment of its kind in Latin America, Bogotá's residents walked, biked, roller skated or took buses and taxis to work on February 24, 2000. But they did not drive.

Nearly 38 years after James Meredith struggled to enter the University of Mississippi (Ole Miss) students elected Nic Latt as the schools' first Black student body president.

Ronald Reagan as President of the United States first veto was to cut spending and vetoed an $85 billion Health and Education Appropriations Bill whose 400 federals programs included on for Alzheimer's research. Reagan subsequently suffered and died from Alzheimer's.

Craig Claiborne was named food editor at the New York Times in 1957. He died on January 22, 2000 and was the first to visit restaurants several times before reviewing them.

Pennsylvania is the ONLY state in the U.S. (i.e. the year 2000) that prohibits local police (state troopers can) from using radar to ticket speeding driver.

Films are probably the ONLY narrative form in history in which the work itself is an incident in a larger drama—the career of a movie god—there must be a body of work reinforcing the star's mythic attributes.

For the first time (2/4/2000) in the Millrose Games 93-year history, the men's sprinters were introduced to the Madison Square Garden crowd with the arena's lights dimmed and spotlights beaming down on them.

On Sunday February 6, 2000 Hillary Rodham Clinton wife of William "Bill" Clinton, President of the United States became the first First Lady to run for official office in the U.S. Government.

Mary Cerat was the first woman executed by the U.S. government.

Patrick T. Harker an award-winning professor at the University of Pennsylvania's Wharton School, has been named dean of the U.S. first collegiate business in February 2000.

ONLY 1 to 2 percent of Americans consume a diet low in fat and high in fruits and vegetables.

Fins (citizens of Finland) elected their first female president Tarja Halonen 2/2/2000 after a tight runoff from former Prime Minister Esko Aho.

The first American Commemorative Quarter of 1893, in uncirculated condition, is now worth almost 10,000 times its face value.

The historic Mapes Hotel in Reno, Nevada, built in 1942, was the first building in the U.S. constructed specifically to house a hotel, casino and live entertainment under one roof. Plans to blow up the hotel on January 30,2000 to expand its riverside district of art galleries, restaurants, etc etc.

The world's first high-tech death cult is getting a face lift besieged by police and the courts; Japan's Aum Supreme Truth apologized for nerve-gassing the Tokyo subway in 1995 and announced that the group is no longer led by Shoko Asahara.

Aleph is the first letter of the Hebrew alphabet.

The American Library Association announced the Bud, not Buddy, Christopher Paul Curtis second novel for young readers, was the first to win both the Newberg Medal and Coretta Scott King Author Award for African-American writers.

Kitty Wells is the first female with a No. 1 country song.

New Hampshire is the ONLY state without a seat belt law as of 2000.

The oath of office of the U.S. president was first taken in New York.

Brooklyn, Ohio, a leafy Cleveland suburb is the first town in the U.S. in which it's illegal to drive and schmooze (talk) on your (hand-held) cell phone at the same time. In 1966 the first mandatory seat-belt law in the U.S. was passed here.

Robert Graves who died in 1985 was an English poet and writer who first achieved notice for his war poetry, but later wrote some of the finest of modern love poems.

The Helioplane is considered the first U.S. short take off and landing craft (STOL).

In the final two minutes of each half in the NFL, ONLY the replay official can challenge a call.

Aaron, brother of Moses was the first priest.

The first new English dictionary—the Encarta World English Dictionary—in 30 years is being billed as more contemporary, more global and more toned-in than the hidebound tomes collecting dust on the shelf.

Hillary Rodham Clinton is credited with being the first First Lady to be burned in effigy.

The combination of New York-based Rogers & Wells and Britain's Clifford Chance, the first marriage of mayor U.S. and British law firms.

The French seer's (Nostradamus) collected prophecies have sold more than six (6) million copies, second ONLY to the Bible. ONLY one of the predictions made by the sixteenth-century mystic has been beyond all question of interpretation.

Papua New Guinea is the ONLY place in the world with a linguistic diversity exceeding West Africa's.

Neil Armstrong, who in 1969 became the first man to set foot on the moon—his feat did not rank among the top 10 engineering achievements of the 20th century.

Cady Stanton an organizer of the first Women's Rights Convention in 1848 paved the way for giving women the right to vote years later.

Utah Gov. Michael O. Leavitt signed a law on March 17,2000 that will make Utah the first state with a pornography czar, a prosecutor who will help local governments restrict or eliminate pornography.

The Oliver Wendell Holmes school—named after the famous Supreme Court Justice—opened in 1917, is the first junior high school in Philadelphia.

On July 25, 1911 Bobby Leach became the first man to make it over Niagara Falls in a barrel.

Created in Lisbon Falls, Maine, in 1884 Moxie became America's first mass-marketed sodey-pop.

Plane crashes are rare—ONLY one per every two million U.S. carrier flights—and 94 percent (94%) of the passengers in all accidents from 1983-86 lived.

India, population which is now one billion, claims 6 percent (6%) of the world's death from auto-related accidents while passing ONLY 1 (1%) of its vehicles—3/2000.

Sally Ride was the first American woman in space.

ONLY 1 percent (1%) of Americans are full time vegetarians, most of them are from the 16-24 age group.

Neurologists studied the brains of taxi drivers in London and the study demonstrates for the first time that a healthy human brain bulks up as it accumulates navigation knowledge.

The star of Ford's 2000 lineup, SuperCrew touts the distinction of being the first half-ton pickup wearing four full-size doors.

Election held in Iran in February 2000 showed hard-liners were ousted from control of the 290-seat Majlis, or Islamic Consultative Assembly, for the first time since the 1979 Islamic revolutions brought the clergy to power.

ONLY teas that come from leaves of the plant Camellia Sinenus—which, in their raw state are brewed to make green tea, and, with curing, can be turned into oolong and black tea leaves—have been shown to contain health benefits.

The laws, which were strongly backed by Gov. Mike Foster and the National Rifle Association (NRA), were passed after New Orleans became the first city in the U.S. to file such a lawsuit in October 1998, claiming gun makers should be held responsible for making a product without adequate safety devices.

The February 1929 edition featured Dr. Fred Merritt Stiles' airborne wedding in "Cupid Turns Pilot". Stiles of Waltham, Massachusetts, became the first Legionnaire to be married in an airplane.

First creature to orbit earth was Laika, a dog, sent up by the Soviet Union on November 3, 1957.

Bob Jones University in Greenville, S.C. have lifted its half-century-old ban on interracial dating, did not admit Blacks until the first Black student was admitted in the 1970s'.

Defense Secretary William S. Cohen traveled to Vietnam in March 2000, becoming the first American defense chief to visit the nation since the Vietnam War.

Alexander Hamilton was the U.S. first treasury secretary.

Katharine Drexel, of Philadelphia, was ONLY the fourth American formally recognized as a saint by the Roman Catholic Church. Saint John Neumann, the fourth Catholic Bishop of Philadelphia, was canonized in 1977.

For the first time, the year 2000 census form allows respondents to mark one or more of 14 boxes representing six races and subcategories or "some other race".

In 2001, the Montefiore Medical Center in the Bronx, New York, opened a children's facility that will be the first space-themed hospital with futuristic explorer passports for patients, a rooftop planetarium, and a video link to NASA's shuttle program.

The $169 (year 2000 price) Sears DieHard Security battery is the first to stop a thief and start your car. If someone tries to start the engine while the system is armed, the battery will not supply power.

"Jazz" is a rare African wildcat—a test-tube baby, born last November '99 at the Audubon Institute Center for research of Endangered Species in New Orleans—the first animal ever born to a mother of another species from a frozen embryo.

The laws of natural genetics pioneered in the 19th century by Austrian monk Gregor Mendel dictate that ONLY like species can interbreed.

Charles Forster invented the first toothpick—making machine in 1869.

Developed by a group led by Hungarian-American physicist Edward Teller, the first thermonuclear device or hydrogen bomb, was exploded at the Eniwetok Atoll in the South Pacific on November 6, 1952.

A new plastic made from plant sugars is expected to become the first such material to be cost-competitive with conventional plastics. Called Natureldorks PLA, the material could be used to make products such as clothing, carpet, cups, etc., etc.

In the year 2000 Texas became the first state that made it legal for young mothers to drop-off their babies at a hospital (safe-place) instead of trashing the child.

Citizens of Arizona were able to vote by the Internet, the first time by voters in the United States—March 11, 2000.

Publisher Simon & Schuster with Stephen King's new book "Riding the Bullet" will be a first for a big-name author and a top publishing house, will be made available exclusively on line March 2000.

The FBI "Ten Most Wanted" started March 14, 1950, Mir Aimal Kansi the Pakistani fugitives wanted for Central Intelligence Agency shootings and Ramzi Yousef, the suspected orchestrator of the World Trade Center bombings, became the first international terrorists place on the list.

Humans are the ONLY animals who drink the milk of other species and who drink milk beyond infancy.

"The Around the World in 80 Days Motor Challenge," of vintage motor cars rally starts in London on May 1, 2000, this will be the first time Westerners have driven across China in their own cars.

Ford Model T was the first motorcar off a moving line.

The first Earth Day was held in 1970.

The SEASTAR is the first pressurized amphibious aircraft that can be built from a kit.

Acknowledging her wartime efforts on their behalf, the people of Volgograd, Russia (4/12/2000) bestowed the citizenship of their city on Queen Mother Elizabeth. It was the first time the award has gone to a non-Russian.

The first permanent English settlement in America was established in 1607 in Jamestown, Va.

The United States did not have a national pavilion at the Expo 2000 in Berlin—the first U.S. absence in the world fair's 149-year history.

Richard Nixon was the first U.S. President to visit the Soviet Union and the ONLY president to resign from office.

Former president Jimmy Carter was selected as the first recipient (April 2000) of the Joint Center for Political and Economic Studies Louis E. Martin Great American Award.

Jeanette Rankin, a Montana Republican was the first woman elected to the House of Representatives in 1916—four years before the 19th amendment was ratified, giving American women the right to vote.

Michael Johnson, a U.S. Navy medic from Arkansas was the ONLY Navy personnel killed in the war to free Iraq in 2003.

Bob Hope's real name is Leslie Towns Hope. In 1941 Hope first performed for U.S. troops. In1992 the U.S. Congress passed a bill naming Hope an Honorary Veteran, the first and ONLY such honor ever bestowed.

Jay Leno in 1992 took over as host of "The Tonight Show" replacing Johnny Carson. Leno's first guest was Billy Crystal.

Pen Hadow began his 480-mile trek on March 17, 2003 from Ward Hunt Island and on May 19, 2003 became the first person to reach the North Pole alone and unaided from Canada.

Virginia Dare became the first English child born in the New World on August 18, 1587.

Explorer VI transmitted the first picture of earth from space on August 7, 1959.

Dorr Eugene Felt patented the first dependable adding machine in October 1817.

On November 3, 1900 31 automakers displayed cars at the first National Auto Show.

On November 16, 1970 Anne Murray became the first Canadian to receive a gold record.

On December 18, 1936 Su-lin became the first panda sent from China to the United States.

Radio City Music Hall opened for the first time in New York City on December 27, 1932.

Ruth Eisemann-Schier was the first woman to make the FBI 10 Most Wanted; seven women have made the list since March 14, 1950.

On July 1, 2000 Washington will become the first state to require that the corrections budget be divvied up based on the risk that ex-offenders represent to the community.

Larry & Jimmy Flint of the famous Hustler magazine opened their first book store in Los Angeles in March 2000 while emphasizing the sale of lingerie.

The first film shown commercially in the United States, "Black Smithing Scene" was made in 1893.

Nationally (US) the first woman executed since 1976 was Velma Bacfield, who died by injection in North Carolina in 1984 for poisoning her boyfriend.

Ice-cream was first served at the World's Fair in Missouri in 1904.

On May 4, 2000 Ken Livingstone "Red "Ken" was elected as the first mayor of London, England.

The first two graduates of West Point Academy, commissioned after seven months, were Joseph Swift, a Christian, and Simon Levy, a Jew.

In 1889 Emily Green Bakh a graduate of Bryn Mawr College, was the first woman to earn the Nobel Peace Prize.

Susan Brandeis Gilbert, a distinguished product of Bryn Mawr College, was the first woman to argue a case before the U.S. Supreme Court—1915.

There has been ONLY one airline, America West, survive out of the 58 that got off the ground between 1978 and 1990.

In April 2000 the FDA okayed Zyvox, the first entirely new type of antibiotic in 35 years.

The U.S. Air Force said on April 5, 2000 it will give new recruits with outstanding college loans up to $10,000 toward repaying their loans. This is the first time in its history that it has offered to help repay college loans of new recruits.

Andres Tischler and a partner opened the nations first "Bed, Bud and Breakfast",—April 2000—a cozy Victorian Inn with a backyard oasis where medical-pot users can fire up right next to the clothing-optional hot tub.

Queen Elizabeth II, first British monarch to speak to the U.S. Congress May 1991.

First printing telegraph-type ticker patented, may 1855.

First automatic electric stock quotation board installed, NYC May 1929.

First narcotic sanatorium patients received, Lexington, Ky. May 1935.

P.T. Barnum and his circus began their first tour, June 1835.

First hovercraft unveiled in England, June 1959.

Fathers Day first observed, June 1910.

First human killed by robot at Jackson, Michigan, July 1984.

First singing telegram "Happy Birthday" sung to Rudy Vallee, July 28, 1933.

First execution using electrocution performed in U.S., in NYC August 1890.

First bowling magazine published in August 1843.

BBC had its first experimental television broadcast (English) August 1932.

First radio commercial broadcast, August 28, 1922.

First U.S. stamp honouring workers issued on September 1, 1956.

First U.S. underground nuclear explosive tested September 1957.

First televised auction of U.S. federal property October 1959.

First women FBI agents complete training, October 1972.

First U.S. man-made major waterway, opened October 1825.

In April 1912 Harriet Quimby became the first woman to fly over the English Channel.

The first Federal income-tax withholding began in 1943.

M. Webb was the first person to swim the English Channel—August 1875.

The first giant squid captured alive, near Bergen Norway—August 1982.

In September 1846, ether was first used as anesthetic.

On October 13,1903 Boston won their first World Series.

In December 1775 the first U.S. flag raised aboard the Alfred.

The first successful flight by the Wright Brothers was on December 17, 1903.

First practical envelope-folding machine patented January 1851.

First dental dispensary opened, NYC February 1791.

First Japanese satellite Osumi launched February 1970.

First U.S. ship to sail to China left NYC February'1784.

First air passenger from U.S. arrived in Alaska on March 17, 1929.

First U.S. patent granted for a washing machine, March 1797.

First surrogate birth of a test-tube baby (a girl) announced, Cleveland April 1986.

First U.S. airmail postage stamps issued, May 1910.

Bahrain, where the first discoveries of oil in the Arab world were made in 1932, now has the smallest oil reserves in the region.

Maine became the first state (May 2000) to decide to use its bargaining power to negotiate prices of prescription medicine for people without coverage.

Books written about Mary, the Mother of Jesus came in seventh place with 3,595 books, and was the ONLY woman in the top 30. Jesus Christ was first with 17,289.

Saline breast implants got its approval in May 2000 from the U.S. Food and Drug Administration, more than 30 years after they first became available.

George Ruggiu, a Belgian-born citizen is the ONLY foreigner to face charges in the 1994 genocide in Rwanda.

In 1936 the League imposed sanctions against Italy and Ethiopia, then known as Abyssinia after Italy invaded. At that time, Ethiopia was the ONLY independent nation in Africa.

The House Ways and Means Committee voted 5/17/2000 to repeal the federal telephone excise tax first imposed in 1898 to help finance the Spanish-American War.

On May 21, 2000, George Bush Sr. was the first U.S. president honoured by the Kennedy Library Foundation with its Distinguished American Award.

Expedition Whydah is a museum on Cape Cod, Massachusetts, that houses artifacts from the first documented pirate ship discovered in the world.

First play-by-play football game broadcast in U.S., Texas A&M 7, University of Texas O, November 1919.

Concentrated milk first sold, November 1950.

First telephone installed the White House, December 1876.

First right-hand-drive auto for mail delivery put in service, December 1951.

Elephant first appeared as symbol for Republican Party in Thomas Nast cartoon, November 1875.

First jukebox installed, San Francisco, November 1869.

First drive-in gas station opened, Pittsburg, Pa, December 1913.

Oberlin College, first coed college, opened, Oberlin, Ohio, December 1833.

First photograph of the moon, December 1839.

First bottled milk delivered, Brooklyn, NY, January 1878.

First commercial jazz recording released, January 1917.

First successful U.S. satellite, Explorer I, launched on January 31, 1958.

John Glenn became first American to orbit the earth, February 20, 1962.

First political cartoon depicting "Uncle Sam" published March 1852.

First dance marathon held in U.S., March 31, 1923.

First "drive-in" movie theatre opened Camden, N.J., June 1933.

First auto seat belt law passed, Illinois, June 1955.

First Lincoln penny issued, August 1909.

First U.S. birth control clinic opened, New York October 1916.

Curtis P. Brady received first permit to drive a car through Central Park, N.Y., November 1889.

Barney Clarke received first artificial heart, December 1982.

Women awarded Rhodes Scholarships for the first time, December 1976.

First Rolling Stone began publication in November 1967.

First recorded auto race in U.S., November 1895.

Christmas Seals first sold to help fight tuberculosis, December 1907.

First Nobel Prizes awarded, December 1901.

First giant panda imported to San Francisco Zoo, December 1936.

Concorde (British and French SST) jet first tested, January 1969.

Oregon became first U.S. state to tax gasoline, February 1919.

Daylight Saving Time first went into effect in U.S., March 1918.

Max Anderson completed first nonstop balloon flight across U.S., May 1980.

Amelia Earhart became first woman to fly solo across the Atlantic, May 1932.

Oil began flowing through the trans-Alaska pipeline for the first time, June 1977.

First street mail boxes installed, Boston and New York, August 1858.

David Brower was the Sierra Club first executive director in the 1950's and 1960's. The Sierra Club was founded in 1892 and as of May 2000 has grown to over 600,000 members.

Woodrow Wilson, 28th president of the U.S. signed in law the ONLY national holiday—Mother's Day—after Congress passed the bill.

The U.S. Military Academy's first general courts-martial for theft in recent memory have been ordered (May 2000) for two cadets,

William Bender and John B. Taylor, charged with felonies in December '99 break-in at West Point's cadet store.

The first five nuclear powers—the United States, Russia, Britain, France and China.

In 1990, Spaniard Jose' Luis Astoreka became the first walnut-cracking world champion, using ONLY his ass in a competition held in the small, friendly village of Kortezubi.

Fred and Wilma Flinstone were the first couple to be shown together in bed on TV.

Q is the ONLY letter that doesn't appear in the name of a U.S. State.

Glenda Ann Bradley, 50 of Cosby, was mauled Sunday, May 21, 2000 becoming the first person killed by a black bear in a federal park or reserve in the Southeast United States.

Joe Engelberger, builder of America's first industrial robot.

First traffic light installed, Cleveland, Ohio, August 1914.

First magnetic video tape recording was produced by Bing Crosby Enterprises, October 1932.

Complete Torah published in English for the first time, October 1952.

First U.S. cross-country airplane flight, November 1911.

Boogie-woogie music first performed at Carnegie Hall, N.Y. December 1938.

Nancy Dickerson, TV reporter who in 1960 became the first woman network correspondent, died October 18, 1997.

Dawn Steel, chair of Columbia Pictures (1987-'91) and the first woman to head a major movie studio, died December 20, 1997.

General Omar Bradley became the first chairman of the Joint Chiefs, August 11, 1949.

The Goldberg's becomes televisions first situation comedy in 1949.

The first Emmy Awards are presented in 1949.

UNICEF sells its first Christmas Cards in 1949.

On November 5, 1974 residents of Washington, DC, for the first time elect their own mayor and city council.

The Philadelphia, Pa. school board voted May 8, 2000 and unanimously requires its 217,000 students to wear uniforms. It is the first big city district in the U.S. to do so.

John Adams was the first U.S. president to practice law.

The United States first great sculptor was William Rush.

An albatross ONLY spends one tenth of its life on land.

The ONLY thing they ever name after a U.S. first lady is a rehab center.

D.B. Cooper, who took over a Northwest Orient Airlines flight on November 24, 1971 demanding $200,000 dollars, is the ONLY one who was ever successful hijacking and nobody knows if he survived.

Diabetes was the first disease that was diagnosed.

North Carolina Museum of Natural Sciences, Raleigh, N.C. houses the first dinosaur found with a fossilized heart and four whale skeletons.

In the late 1800's, Martha Matilda Harper, a 5-foot-tall domestic with floor-length hair created what a new biography calls America's first retail franchise: Harper Hair Dressing Salons. Martha designed the first reclining shampoo chair and a sink with a cutout lip for the neck to rest.

Costa Rico is the first country to offer all its citizens free E-mail.

When it was first written the title of the classic song "Happy Birthday to You" was "Good Morning to All".

San Francisco's famed Presidio which played a major role in many of America's wars; it's the ONLY national park in the U.S. being required by Congress to pay for itself.

Citigroup Inc. in Banking and Credit:

> First U.S. bank to establish a foreign department.
> First U.S. nations bank to open a foreign branch.
> First savings account offering compound interest.
> First unsecured personal loans to depositors.
> First U.S. bank to reach $1 billion in assts.
> First "leveraged lease" to finance jet aircraft.
> First U.S. bank with branches in all nine Common Market countries.
> First floating-rate notes.
> First "stretch" mortgages.
> First automobile loan in the United States
> First negotiable Certificate of Deposit.

Citigroup Inc in Insurance:

> First accident insurance policy.
> First double indemnity policy.
> First automobile insurance policy.
> First Corps of Safety Engineers.
> First aircraft liability insurance.
> First TV commercial for insurance.
> First accident policies for space flight and lunar Exploration.
> First insurance office of consumer information.
> First quote-to-issue automobile policies over the internet.

"THE RICH GET RICHER AND THE POOR GET POORER TRYING TO GET RICH"

The Hubble Space Telescope, which itself is considered second ONLY to Galileo's first telescope in 1610 for its impact on astronomy.

Jose Cuervo launched its first Spanish-language advertisement in 2003 for America's fastest-growing liquor. Cuervo is the largest tequila producer in Mexico.

Gen. James L. Jones is the first U.S. Marine to serve as NATO's Supreme Allied Commander, Europe.

Jack Daniel distilled his first batch of whiskey at age nine.

Barbara Streisand has an astounding 50 gold albums (second ONLY to Elvis a/o 2003) and 28 platinum albums—more than any other woman.

In 1988 Northwest Airlines became the first U.S. airline to ban smoking on all domestic flights.

Benazir Bhutto of Pakistan became the first woman in 1988 in a predominantly Moslem country to become head of state.

Howard Dean became (November '03) the first Democratic presidential candidate to reject taxpayer money and avoid the accompanying spending limits. No major-party candidate has ever skipped public financing in the general election.

Volvo's Four-C system, found on the 2000 S60R and V70R, is the ONLY traction-control scheme that prevents slippage by actively anticipating it.

Joseph Gruver received his Eagle Scout badge in 1929 becoming Bucks County, Pa first Eagle Scout.

America's first comprehensive antismoking ordinance was passed in 1977 in Berkeley, California.

The Luxuriant Flowing hair Club for Scientists—the first member was Steven Pinker an MIT scientist where long, curly locks are reminiscent of Isaac Newton's.

The Tag Hever V4 is the first wristwatch ever to run on drive belts. Automatic watches ordinarily use dozens of gears to power movement but belts are more efficient because they cut out the friction inherent in a chain of cogs.

The RolleiFlex Mini-Digi is the first twin-lens reflex digicam that let you watch the action happen through one lens—on an LCD screen on top.

The Casio A5406CA is the world's first 3.2 mp camera phone that has 12.8 MB of memory.

The Zap MBZ heavy-duty minibike is the first AWD off-road electric minibike.

The ERS-7 robot is the first model that talks with a human-sounding voice, but its annoyingly chipper.

Edward B. Lewis, Nobel-prizewinning geneticist died July 2004 of cancer. He was 81. Using the lowly fruit fly, the Caltech professor was the first to explain how genes control the growth of a fertilized egg into a fully developed embryo.

Filmmaker—Michael Moore's Fahrenheit 9/11 grossed over $100 million dollars in 2004—a first for a documentary film.

Maggots are getting more attention these days. In January 2004, they became the first live animals to win Food and Drug Administration approval—as a medical device to clean out wounds.

Paul Conklin was the Peace Corp's first official photographer.

Lloyd Scott emerged from Loch Ness, Scotland on October 9, 2003 after completing the world's first underwater marathon.

Iranian dissident Hashem Aghajari became the first Moslem woman to win the Nobel Peace Prize—2003. She also was the first Iranian female judge before the 1979 Revolution.

Judith Scruggs, mother of J. Daniel Scruggs was convicted in October 2003 of one felony count of risk of injury to a minor for creating an unhealthy, unsafe home environment that contributed to suicide. Scruggs was the first parent in the state (Connecticut)—maybe the country—to be convicted in connection with her child's suicide.

China launched its first satellite in 1970—which broadcast back to Earth the Maoist anthem The East Is Red—but that program suffered a string of disastrous explosions in the mid-1990's.

Lt. Col. Yang landed by parachute on the grasslands of Inner Mongolia in northern China on October 15, 2003 to become China's first astronaut.

Polish Cardinal Karol Wojtyla was elected Pope John Paul II in October 1978 the first non-Italian pope in 455 years.

Great Britain's first Prime Minister was Sir Robert Walpole.

North America's ONLY legal government sponsored safe injection site is in downtown Vancouver, British Columbia. The trial project was opened in September 2003.

The Massachusetts State Supreme Court ruled that marriages between gay couples are legal (November 18, 2003), thus becoming the first state in the U.S. recognizing and making gay marriages legal.

Spencer Percival is the ONLY British Prime Minister to have been assassinated.

Michael Douglas received the Cecil B. DeMille Award for career achievement at the 2003 Golden Globes, more than three decades after his father, Kirk Douglas, won the honour in 1968. Michael is the first second-generation actor to receive the DeMille Award.

Colgate began marketing its first toothpaste commercial brand in 1873.

The USS Vandegrift paid a visit to Ho Chi Minh City in November 2003, becoming the first U.S. Warship to visit postwar Vietnam.

Europe's Airbus A380 is the first fully double-decked passenger jet, will take flight in 2006 and seats 555 passengers in three classes.

President George Bush made a secret and surprise visit to Iraq on Thanksgiving Day in 2003 to visit troops. This was the first time a U.S. president had ever visited Iraq.

Margaret Gorman, the first Miss America was crowned on national (U.S.) television in 1954.

Jan Davis was the first woman to successfully jump (parachute) from the lip of the Angel Falls in Venezuela which is over 3,000 feet.

A hundred years after the end of their legendary feud the Hatfield's and the McCoy's are getting together on the weekend of May 10, 2000 for their first reunion.

Researchers measuring the rate of genetic change in HIV, the virus that causes AIDS, found the current strains originated from a common master that first evolved from a simian virus in Southeast Africa between 1915 and 1941, with1931 the most likely year.

The first murderer as mentioned in the Bible was Cain. What was the weapon?

Barnum & Bailey Circus made their first appearance at Madison Square Garden in New York City in 1919.

The Son of Beast wooden roller coaster at Paramount's King Island in Ohio is the first looping wooden roller coaster in the world.

A new seismic hazard map, produced by the International Lithosphere Program with support from the United Nations International Decade for Natural Hazards Reduction, the first map to show the entire planet's earthquake hazard zones.

Curt Floodworth became the first person to be exonerated by DNA.

The first "flags" consisted of symbols attached to the tops of poles. Such flag like objects appear in Egyptian art in the mid-3000's B.C.

A dollar coin has turned up in Arkansas (June 3, 2000) with the front of a George Washington quarter and the back of a Sacagawea dollar: It is believed to mark the first error of its kind in the Mint's 208-year history—and the coin would fetch as much as $100,000 at auction.

In June 2000 a South Vietnamese's remains were brought back from Vietnam and buried beside his wife creating the first military cemetery (Orange County) for South Vietnamese soldiers and their spouses outside their homeland.

Indian, founded in 1901 as America's first motorcycle company—three years before Harley-Davidson—Indian broke down in the 50's and didn't recover.

Lucy Hayes was the first First Lady with a college degree.

Ed White was the first American astronaut to walk in space.

Franklin Delano Roosevelt (FDR) was the first U.S. president to tape record meetings, especially news conferences.

In 1864 "In God We Trust" first appeared on an American coin.

Tuna fish was first canned in 1903.

Playboy's first Key Club opened in Chicago in 1960.

The U.S. Department of Energy's Waste Isolation Pilot Plant (WIPP), the world's first underground repository for radioactive garbage.

The very first wearable computing device—the clock—is now most commonly worn on the wrist.

The first known bird, Archeopteryx, appeared about 145 million years ago, some 75 million after the date for Longisquama, (i.e. the fossil of a small lizard-like, flying reptile with a complex set of feathers).

In 1846 an Englishman named Fred Russell, the father of modern ventriloquism, became the first man known to seat a puppet on his knee.

The first transatlantic image transmitted on television in 1925 was of a ventriloquial head named Bill.

Italian scientists have for the first time (June 2000) transplanted human ovarian tissue into a mouse, extracted eggs and made them potentially fertilizable.

ONLY residents may fish this sanctuary in American Samoa, the first U.S. national park in the Southern Hemisphere.

In June 2000 the state of New York filed suit claiming gun manufacturers and wholesalers created "a condition of danger", making it the first state to sue the firearms industry.

Stand-up comic Margaret Cho, the first Asian-American star of her own sitcom, All-American Girl.

Capt Cynthia Anderson became the first woman to stand guard at Buckingham Palace, London, when she led a unit in the morning parade July 1, 2000, part of a company of Australian soldiers who have temporarily taken over protection duties from the usual all-male British Guard.

The years 1700, 1800 and 1900 were not leap years, but 2000 is a leap year, the first century leap year since 1600.

In July of the year 2000 Vincent Fox was elected president of Mexico for six years, the first time in more than a century an opposition candidate has done so.

Omega is the ONLY brand of watch that's been worn on the moon.

A federal judge has struck down (July 2000) the U.S. first local ATM fee bans, those approved in the fall of 1999 by San Francisco voters and Santa Monica's City Council.

Starbucks first made a humble start at Pike's Place Market in 1971, the green and white Starbucks sign is visible on more than 3,000 Starbucks worldwide, 144 in the greater Seattle area and 78 in Seattle alone in the year 2000.

For the first time we have a 50 milligram pill (Viagra) that in less than an hour will put the starch back in any man's romantic inklings.

The first steam-powered vehicle is a 1763 carriage by a Frenchman named Cugnot.

In July 2000, along with Surgeon General David Satcher and the Federal Trade Commission, the seven leading cigar makers for the first time agreed to put health warnings on cigar packages and in ads.

The Gothic Revival house, built in 1842 by George Riggs of Riggs National Bank, lies three miles north of the White House. In

1851, it became the U.S. first home for disabled, retired veterans, before being used by presidents from 1857-1884 as a summer cottage.

The world's first trimaran warship concept, the PVTriton, has been launched by the United Kingdoms' Defense Evaluation and Research Agency—year 2000.

The Rev. Vashti McKenzie was elected on Tuesday, July 11, 2000 to become the first bishop of the 2 million-member African—Methodist Episcopal Church.

In the year 2000 there were ONLY four states mandated that human evolution be taught in schools.

News Helicopters first gained popularity in California and their use has spread nationwide.

The Chesapeake & Ohio No. 614, is the last steam passenger locomotive built in the U.S., and it's the ONLY steam locomotive in North America that has all the equipment and appliances you'd need to pull and Amtrak train.

Betty Boothroyd is the first woman to serve as speaker of Britain's House of Commons, she was elected speaker in 1992. The Labour Party member was the first speaker to dispense with wearing a long white wig.

Captain James Cook on January 17, 1773, his ship, the Resolution, and its companion, the Adventure, were the first vessels known to cross the Antarctic Circle.

Antarctica is the ONLY continent on earth to be completely governed by an international agreement called the Antarctic Treaty.

A snakebite serum manufactured by Wyeth-Ayerst Laboratories is the ONLY product available (July 2000) to naturalize toxins from three types of poisonous North American snakes: rattlesnakes, cottonmouths and copperheads.

Queen Elizabeth II opened the new British Embassy in Berlin, Germany (July 2000) thus becoming the first British monarch to open an embassy.

Vladimir Putin paid the first-ever visit by a Russian president to communist North Korea on July 19, 2000, meeting with leader Kim Jong II.

Champagne first became available in 1698, when Dan Pierre Perignon perfected the art of fermenting wine in the bottle at the abbey of Hautvillers in Champagne, France.

Al Lapin Jr. built the first blue-roofed International House of Pancakes (IHOP) in Los Angeles in 1958 and turned the business into a $40 million conglomerate by 1970.

The French company Ricarimpex SAS is the first to have sought and received FDA clearance, under a 1976 law, to market the invertebrates (leeches) for medicinal purposes.

Karol Kennedy Kucher, half of the figure-skating duo known as the Kennedy Kids, who became the first American pair to win a world championship when they captured the gold in London in 1950.

Margarine was first patented on July 15, 1869.

The Rolling Stones played their first gig in 1962 at a club in London.

The WHO began their first U.S. tour in 1967, opening for Herman's Hermit in Seattle.

Don Tosti who died in August 2004, was the fusion of boogie blues, swing and Latin beats that propelled him to become the first Latin artist to sell a million records in the U.S.

Starbucks, the Seattle-based coffee company opened its first store in Paris, France in January 2004. Starbucks have a world-wide policy—no smoking in all its stores. Starbucks first entered the European market in 1998 with a store in Britain. Worldwide, the company serves 25million to 30 million customers a week, making it the most frequented retail chain in the world.

In 1946 Robert Fulton designed and built the Airphibian, the first "roadable" plane certified by the Civil Aeronautics Administration. Eleven Airphibians would be built in the 1950's before Fulton's Company ran out of money.

On Friday July 28, 2000 L.L. Bean opened a 75,000-foot anchor store at Tyson's Corner Center Mall in the suburbs of Washington D.C., it will be Beans first major store outside of Maine.

Emirates, the flag carrier of the United Arab Emirates, was the first airline to officially commit to the Airbus Industries A3XX double-decker jumbo 555 passenger jet.

The British and French SST Concorde is the ONLY aircraft that has flown passengers at super sonic speed. The Concorde after nearly three decades of flying had their first crash on Tuesday July 25, 2000 in Paris, France, killing 99 people on board and four on the ground. The British and French stop flying the Concorde in 2003 because of economical reasons.

Adenovirus-36, discovered in July 2000, is the first human virus that has been shown to cause obesity in animals, and it is the first human virus known to cause an increase in fat.

On June 16, 1903 Ford Motor Company filed articles of incorporation in Lansing, Michigan. One week later, the first production car, a two-cylinder Model A was sold.

John W. Tukey, a Princeton University statistician is the first person credited with coining the word software; he died Wednesday July 26, 2000 at age 85.

The Chinese claimed to have unearthed the world's first flush toilet at a dig in Central China. Dated about 206 B.C., it is reportedly much like what we are using today.

The first-ever Shadow Convention July 3, 2000-August 3, 2000 a crosstown alternative to the Republican National Convention, Philadelphia, Pa, was called a success by attendees and its organizer Arianna Huffington, to syndicated columnist and author of "How to Overthrow the Government".

High demand and tight supplies mean higher prices—particularly in San Diego, California, the first area in the United States to purchase power in the open market.

Rising transportation and labour costs forced Ringling Brothers to close its tent flaps for the last time on July 19, 1956, at the Heidelberg Racetrack South of Pittsburg, Pa. Ringling Brothers circus tents are being raised again for the first time in 44 years for Barnum's Kaleidoscope, an intimate one-ring show.

The Delaware Bay is the ONLY place in the world where the arrival of shore birds and horseshoe crabs coincides.

Vice-president Al Gore selected as his running mate Senator Joseph Lieberman (August 7, 2000)—the Senator from Connecticut is the first Jew on a major-party ticket for a presidential election. Although Lieberman voted against impeachment for President Clinton he was the first Democrat to chastise the president for the affair with Monica Lewinsky, branding it "immoral".

Birds, turtles, fish, primates and some lizards are the ONLY animals with backbones that can see colour. Deer ONLY see shades of gray.

Venezuelan President Hugo Chavez, on a tour of fellow members of the Organization for the Exporting Countries (OPEC), visited Iraq on August 10, 2000. Chavez was be the first head of state to visit Iraq an meet President Saddam Hussein since the 1991 Persian Gulf War that ejected Iraqi troops from Kuwait.

The world's first digital camcorder to record directly to DVD-CAM, Hitachi's DVD-RAM camcorder stores up to 2 hours of high-quality MPEG-2 video.

The first saw to use a built-in computer to monitor rotational speed, Rotozip's Revolution provides your needs to maintain a clean, smooth cut.

Braun's Syncro System offers the cleanest clean shave; the dry shave razor is the first that actually washes itself.

NEON Technology's internet DVD player is the first to combine Internet access with DVD player that has built-in Dolby Digital decoding.

Ellen DeGeneres was the first openly gay lead on American television.

Submarines:

> The first submarine, the Turtle dates back to 1775.
> The U.S. Navy buy its first submarine, U.S.S. Holland, from John Holland.
> The U.S.S. Porpoise is the first all electric-drive Submarine—1933.
> In 1953 the U.S.S. Albacore is the first to use a teardrop hull design for higher speed as well as the First fiberglass sonar dome.
> In 1955 the first nuclear-power sub, the U.S.S. Nautilus.
> In 1960 the U.S.S. George Washington launches the first Polaris missiles with a range of 1,200 miles.

The first patent for any type of lawn-mowing device was granted to an inventor in England in 1830.

Willis Carrier designed the first air conditioner in 1902. His first customer was a Brooklyn, New York printer.

Christopher Latham Sholes invented the first operative typewriter in 1868; it was arranged in alphabetical order.

The Muppet Show was first aired on TV on September 13, 1976.

Hilary Koprowski oversaw the first mass inoculation with an oral polio vaccine, in the Belgian Congo in 1958, and was actually the first to test such a vaccine on humans.

NASA scientists for the first time (August 2000) tracked tiny, high-speed particles from a rocket that exploded in space.

The first Ronald Reagan Film Festival (2/26/2000), a trail that follows President Reagan's early life runs through Tampico, where he was born, and Eureka College, where he went to school.

Fox Chase Cancer Center was honoured by the American Nursing Association for outstanding nursing (August2000)—making the center the first hospital in Pennsylvania and the first cancer specialty hospital in the U.S. to receive such recognition.

Farmers Almanac predictions of the weather using the formula which is based on sunspots, the position of the planets and tidal action caused by the moon—formula is known ONLY to two people.

Chuck Berry's first hit "Maybellene", topped the R&B Country and Western, and pop charts.

A computer programmed to follow the rules of evolution has for the first time (August 2000) designed and manufactured simple robots with minimal help form people.

At least two people in the West are believed to have contracted Legionnaires disease from potting soil in the first (August 2000) such cases ever reported in the United States.

ONLY in Jamaica, West Indies, you'll have police cars parked up at some rum bar.

The first drive-in theater was opened in Camden, N.J., in 1933, by Richard M. Hollingshead who developed the ramped parking that made it possible for movie goers to see the screen over the car ahead.

Norway's popular Crown Prince Haakon plans to move in with his girlfriend, a single mother which would make him the first European prince to openly live with a girlfriend without being married.

The U.S. Secret Service made its first request for a e-mail wire tap in 1995, and its first pager intercepts in 1997, before the FBI began using the controversial Carnivore technology to monitor e-mail via a suspect's Internet Service Provider.

In September 2000 the Iranian Islamic Republic News Agency reported that American and Iranian lawmakers met for the first time since the 1979 Islamic revolution.

In 1999 Sega Dreamcast became the first home video game system with a modem inside.

The World's First Modern Elephant was founded in 1994 by Soraida Salwala, a passionate conservationist Thai.

Evangeline Villegas, a cereal chemist scientist is the first woman to receive the World Food Prize (September 2000), the prize was established by Nobel Peace Prize winner Norman E. Borlaug.

The return of illegal Chinese by Taiwan (September 8, 2000) was the first repatriation of Chinese returned to Mainland China.

U.S. District Court Judge George A. O'Toole of Boston has declared the nation's first law (September 2000) requiring tobacco companies to list the ingredients of their products unconstitutional, saying it forces the companies to give away their trade secrets.

Gael Greene wrote the New York magazine first restaurant review in October 1968.

The Federal Correctional Institution in Dublin, California, the low-level security prison where Sara Jane More is serving a life sentence for trying to assassinate President Gerald Ford in 1975, is the U.S. ONLY federal women's prison that allows inmates to lock their own cells.

In 1872 Eadweard Muybridge devised a technique for taking the first high-speed movies.

The first factory in Europe to produce porcelain was established in Meissen, Germany in 1710.

In 1828, Andrew Jackson became the first presidential candidate to run as the head of an organization that called itself the Democratic Party. When the Democrats wanted to nominate "Old Hickory" for a second term, they met in Baltimore for the first national convention of the Democratic Party.

In the early 1950's Frank Mather designed the first tag still used in most marine fisheries research today.

The Scots cloned a sheep called Dolly, which was the first use of cells from an adult mammal to clone another animal.

Christian Marty was the pilot that got killed when the first Concorde SST crashed in Paris, he was also the first Frenchman ever to wind surf across the Atlantic.

The SOLAR SAILOR is the first sun-and-wind-powered catamaran, carries up to 100 passengers; the vessel uses solar panels to capture sunlight for power.

Queen Elizabeth II was given a new Bentley state limousine to mark her 50 years on the throne in 2002, the car will be the Queen's first Bentley, taking its place in a stable of Rolls-Royces.

Jennifer Murray, a British grandmother completed (September 2000) and became the first woman to fly solo around the world in a helicopter, clocking 21,750 miles in a flight that spanned 30 countries.

When television first entered our living rooms, Archbishop Fulton Sheen became not just a voice, but a face, the first to combine the force of religion and a mesmerizing new medium.

For the first time in 36 years (year 2000), Cadillac is modifying its familiar wreath-and-crest logo in another step to shake its stodgy image.

The jury took ONLY eleven (11) minutes to find Dennis "Leppo" Lobban, the man that killed Jamaican reggae star Peter Tosh guilty. One of the fastest jury convictions under British Judiciary System.

Five U.S. Congressional staff members ignored State Department objections (8/29/99), by beginning a fact-finding mission to Iraq, the first such journey since the 1991 Persian Gulf War.

ONLY once in the history of "The Price is Right" TV daytime show two contestants won $11,000 dollars each—show aired September 11,2000.

The man (Jesse Timmendequas) whose rape and murder of a neighbor prompted Megan's Law is getting his second mandatory Supreme Court appeal (September 2000), the first such review since the court ordered changes in how death sentences are examined.

A ship that replaces compressed-air and hydraulic systems with electrically driven, called Integrated Power System, the first ship to use the system, is expected to set sail in 2000.

Hillary Rodham Clinton triumphed (Tuesday November 2000) in her historic quest for the U.S. Senate, defeating Republican Rick Lazio in the N.Y. Senatorial race to become the ONLY first lady ever elected to public office.

Traditional hearing aids amplify all sound—whether it's street noise or a doctor's instructions. Phonok's Claro is the first hearing-assist device to adjust automatically to either quiet or noisy environments by analyzing the sound source.

Jacuzzi's two-person "Affinity" is the first whirlpool bath with a built-in television and CD stereo system.

The 2002 Buick Rendezvous, the GM division's first sport-utility vehicle and first truck-based vehicle of any sort since 1923.

On Tuesday September 12, 2000 Hillary Rodham Clinton became the first First Lady to win any election in the United States.

This is the first time (2000) in 188 years that all four presidential and vice presidential candidates have attended Ivy League Schools:

> Harvard for Al Gore, and Yale for George Bush, Joe Lieberman, and Dick Cheney.

The first live pay-per-listen Webcast was August 17, 2000.

Michael Smith was the first U.S. Ambassador to the General Agreement on Tariff's and Trades (GATT).

For the first time (September 17, 2000), an Academy Award was auctioned online—the best-actor statuette James Cagney won for playing George M. Cohan in the 1942 movie "Yankee Doodle Dandy".

The first three digits of a Social Security Number (SSI) indicate the geographic location—state or zip code—of residences when the card was issued.

The Vatican on September 26, 2000 defended its decision to canonize 120 Roman Catholics killed in China. Eighty-seven of them are the first Chinese ever raised in Sainthood.

Carly Fiorina, former president and chief executive officer (September 2000) of Hewlett-Packard Co., was named to the additional post of chairman, becoming the first woman to have all three top posts at a major computer company.

The U.S. Ambassador to Israel, Martin Indyk, was under FBI investigation, the first American Ambassador to be stripped of his security clearances—year 2000.

New York immigration attorney Robert Porges was charged with helping to smuggle Chinese immigrants to the U.S. by the Immigration and Naturalization Service (INS). Porge's case is the first to invoke the Civil Asset Forfeiture Reform Act of 2000.

In 1990 the "Africanized" killer bees first jumped the border into the U.S.

After the California Air Resource Board mandated that manor automakers had to offer so-called zero-emission electric cars by 1997, GM was the first to comply, with the $33,995 EVI. ONLY 747 were sold.

The World Wrestling Federation (WWF) champ The Rock (real name Dwayne Johnson) signed a $5.5 million (September 2000) deal with Universal Pictures to star as the action hero in "The Scorpion King" a spin-off of the up coming "The Mummy 2: It's one of the highest amounts paid an actor in his first starring role.

The Harlem Globetrotters appeared in their first comedy movie, Alan Sandler's "Little Nicky" in the fall of 2000.

In an extraordinary clash between church and state (September 2000), a federal judge ordered a congregation to clear out of its church to satisfy a nearly $6 million dept to the IRS. A first of its kind in the United States.

The Organization of Petroleum Exporting Countries (OPEC) wrapped up its summit on September 28, 2000 in Caracas, Venezuela; this was ONLY the second summit of OPEC's 40-year history.

Prince William of England gave his first news conference on September 29, 2000. During the conference he addressed the exploitation of his Mothers name, Princess Di. She died in a car crash 1997.

The year 2001 GMC Sierra C3, the first half-ton pick-up with a 6 liter engine and AW.D.

The English game of field hockey was introduced to American women in 1901. It was considered the ONLY vigorous sport proper for women.

St. Michael's Indian Mission School, on a Navajo reservation in St. Michael's, Arizona, founded in 1902, it includes the first high school for Navajo Indians.

Every new handgun sold in Maryland (effective October 1, 2000), the manufacturer will have to give state police a spent shell casing carrying the weapons ballistic fingerprint—the first of its kind in the United States.

ONLY in Jamaica citizens have to protect police from gunmen—year 2000.

Twenty seven million people watched the first televised Miss America Pageant in 1954.

It was Galileo who first demonstrated that sunspots actually rotate across the surface of the sun.

Dr. Nathaniel Kleitman (1895-1999) was the first to gather information on slumber, with his students to identify sleep's different stages.

Annie Taylor made the first historic trip over the Niagara Falls in 1901.

The pioneering Soul Stirrers, the first gospel group inducted into the Rock 'N Roll Hall of Fame.

Motels were introduced first in the U.S. in 1925; each room had a parking space outside your door.

Noah is a gaur, an ox like creature, the first endangered animal ever cloned.

First federal prisoners arrived at Alcatraz on August 11, 1934.

The newly elected Speaker of the House of Commons Michael Martin became the first (October 2000) male in the Commons to rid himself of a wig rather than acquire one.

The shark is the ONLY fish that can blink with both eyes.

Doctors at a Veterans Affairs Pittsburg Healthcare System hospital performed bypass surgery (October 2000) on a 51-year-old patient who was awake (epidermal anesthetic) and talking during the procedure. It was the first time such a surgery had been performed in the United States.

The first U.S. animal in orbit was Ham, a chimpanzee, January 31, 1961.

The first published drawing by Robert L. Ripley of "Believe It Or Not" appeared in the New York Globe December 19, 1918.

The movie "The Law of the Range" in 1911 is said to be the first Hollywood-produced picture.

The "USS Birmingham" a U.S. Navy cruiser from which the first airplane took off November 14, 1910, piloted by Eugene Ely, a civilian.

Buddy was the name of the first Seeing Eye dog in America, brought to the U.S. in 1928 from Switzerland by owner Morris Frank.

In 1926 Richard E. Byrd, a Navy Captain, was the first to fly over the North Pole.

Captain (Christopher) Pike was the first commander of the Starship "Enterprise": first called Captain April, then Captain Water, and then Pike.

The Titanic was the first ship to use SOS the night she sank in April 1912. There were ONLY four women alive from that disaster as of January 2001.

The British ship "Carpathia" was the first to answer the SOS of the "Titanic", they picked up 705 survivors. David Sarnoff received the SOS.

ONLY two years in which the U.S. had three (3) presidents:

1841:

Martin Van Buren (Until March 3rd)
William Henry Harrison (died April 4th, one month after
    Inauguration.
John Tyler (April 6th-March 3rd, 1845).

1881:

Rutherford Birchard Hayes (until March 3rd).
James Abram Garfield (March 4th—shot July 2nd—died
    September 19th.
Chester Alan Arthur (September 19th-March 3, 1885)

The first ten members elected to the Entertainment Hall of Fame
1974:

Tennessee Williams, Charlie Chaplin, Katharine
Hepburn, Irving Berlin, Judy Garland, Lawrence Olivier,
George Gershwin, D.W. Griffith, Eugene O'Neill and
George Bernard Shaw.

American Astronaut Bill Shephard and his Russian crew
mates Yuri Gidzenko and Serget Krikalev rocketed into space
October 31, 2000 on a quest to become the first residents of the
international space station.

The 4th largest circus in the world—the Suarez Brothers Circus
from Mexico brought to the Caribbean in October 2000 the first
time in history the Polar Bears.

Lindley Troy Geborde, the man accused of organizing the
party and supplying the designer drug GHB (date-rape-drug)
to 15 year-old Luvas Biolet went on trial November 6, 2000 for

second-degree murder in what may be the first such case in the United States.

The first real innovation in handwriting since 1922 came in 1974, when Charles Lehman's Simple Italic Handwriting, a teachers guide was chosen as one of the official public-school texts in Oregon.

The ONLY English work with a triple letter: goddessship.

The ONLY word in which an "f" is pronounced like a "V": OF.

Navy Rear Admiral Grace Hopper "Amazing Grace", was a programmer on the first large-scale digital computer. She built the first A-O compiler, which went live on November 4, 1952.

In 1954 the French produce the world's first nonstick Teflon frying pan.

The first United States sentry dog (Chips) sent overseas during World War II: awarded Silver Star and Purple Heart.

First Lady of the Screen—nickname of actress Norma Shearer.

First Lady of the Theatre—nickname of actress Helen Hayes.

The first recorded message "Mary had a little lamb": by Thomas Edison in 1877, his assistant, Mrs. Harriet Atwood, played the piano, thus becoming the first recording artist.

Hoot Gibson, cowboy actor, real name Edward Richard claimed to have been Hollywood's first stuntman.

Jean Harlow was the first female movie star to appear on the cover of Life Magazine.

Idaho is the ONLY state in the U.S. over which no foreign flag has ever flown.

"I Wanna Be Your Man" was the ONLY song written and recorded by The Beatles which was also performed by The Rolling Stones.

The first ship to take on oil from the Alaskan Pipeline at Valdez, Alaska was ARCO tanker "Juneau" on August 1, 1977.

William Kemmler on August 6, 1890 became the first person to be executed in the electric chair.

Miss Columbia was the name given to the first airplane purchased by the U.S. government from the Wright Brothers in August 1909.

John Hancock was the first signer of the Declaration of Independence, and the ONLY one to actually sign on July 4, 1776.

The Beatles came to the U.S. on Pan American flight #101 and arrived at JFK International on February 7, 1964 for their first American tour.

The first Republican candidate for president was John C. Fremont (1830-1890) nickname the Pathfinder.

Pepsi Cola (NENCN-KONA in Russia) was the first consumer product for sale in the U.S.S.R.

In April 1967 Shirley Preston became the first female taxicab driver in London, England.

Lt. Gen. Lewis B. Puller is the ONLY marine to win 5 Navy Crosses.

The Pulitzer Prize is for awards in journalism, creative writing, music and related areas, the first award was made in 1917.

The "Question Mark" was the name of the first plane to fly non-stop from Europe to the United States on September 2, 1930.

Hugo Gernsback who coined the words Science Fiction is the founder of Amazing Stories (1926) the first fiction magazine.

The first Cinema Scope movie was "The Robe" by 20th Century-Fox in 1953 starring Richard Burton.

The first airplane fatality in the world happened on September 17, 1908 at Fort Myers, Virginia when Lt. Thomas E. Selfridge was killed.

'Singing in the Rain" was the ONLY movie in which Gene Kelly and Donald O'Connor appeared together—1952.

Timmie Jean Lindsey of Houston, Texas was the first person to have a Silicone breast implant in 1962.

Motorola DynaTAC 8000 cell phone—the "brick phone" was the world's first (1985) commercial hand-held cell, weighed in at roughly two pounds and cost consumers a measly $3,995.

Robert Dewitt died in December 2003; he was an Episcopal Bishop who upset the church hierarchy by taking part in the first ordination of women as priests in 1974.

Auntie Anne's grew from a pretzel stand first opened in 1988 by Annie Beiler who was raised in an Amish Mennonite family in Lancaster County. The first international store opened in 1995 in Jakarta, Indonesia.

Charles Lindbergh in 1927 was Time Magazine's first Person of the Year Award.

Yuri Malenchenko, the Russian Cosmonaut didn't let the fact that he's living (2003) aboard the International Space Station stop him from marrying his earthbound bride, Ekaterina Dmitriev, about 240 miles below, in the first wedding ever conducted from space.

Dr. Guy Hugh Chan was the Chairperson of Ophthalmology at Temple University from 1978 to 1993 and the first person of Chinese origin to attain the position of Chairperson of Ophthalmology at an academic medical center in the United States.

Sony's Aibo was the first major toy that tapped microelectro-mechanical systems (MEMS) technology.

General Henry "Hap" Arnold, a West Point graduate, military career spanned two World Wars. Arnold retired in March 1946, but returned to service in 1949 when President Truman gave him the first-ever United States commission to rank of Permanent Five-star General of the Air Force.

Richard E. Byrd began the second expedition to Antarctica from 1933 to 1935. The first human voices were transmitted from base camp known as Little America II, on February 1, 1934, and weekly broadcasts followed.

Louise Thaden was the first woman to win the Bendix Trophy Race in 1936, piloted a Staggerwing, while other contestants chose to compete using sleeker monoplanes.

The B-47 Stratojet, the world's first swept-wing jet bomber, made its debut in 1947.

The U.S. lost the carrier Lexington, and the Japanese lost the Soho. This was the first naval (WWII) battle in history in which opposing ships did not see or fire upon each other—the attacks were carried out by the airplanes from the carriers.

America's first peacetime draft was instituted with the Selective Training and Service Act of 1940. The draft continued, with modifications, during time of peace and conflict until 1973, when the United States converted to an all-voluntary military.

The first legislation of its kind, the GI Bill (1944) provided veterans with education and training; home, farm and business loans.

General John L. Hines, in WWI was awarded The Distinctive Service Cross for extraordinary heroism during the Battle of Soissons. He also was the ONLY commander to lead a regiment, Brigade, division, and corps in combat during that war.

Danny Kaye was the first U.N. goodwill ambassador.

Warren Kremer, lead cartoonist for Harvey Comics who with the company's editor and publisher, created Richie Rich, the "poor little rich boy" was first introduced in 1953. Kremer died in September 2003. He was 82.

Johnny Cash who died in September 2003 released his first single in 1955—"Hey Porter" with "Cry, Cry, Cry" on the flip side.

Oberlin Collegiate Institute became the first coeducational college in the U. S. in 1833.

Eugene Ely was the first person to land a plane on a ship—January 1911.

"Uncle Sam" appeared in cartoon for the first time on March 13, 1852.

Bryan Allen was the first person to cross the English Channel in a pedal-powered aircraft in June 1979.

John Tyler was the first U.S. President to marry while in office on June 23, 1844.

Somporn Saekow, founder of the first Thailand monkey-training school died on august 20, 2002.

Sun-Times published the first Ann Landers column by Eppie Lederer in October of 1955.

Doris Hansen received the 2003 Trucker of the Year Award. Hansen is the first woman to be so honored. She logged more than 800,000 miles of driving in 31 years without an accident.

The littorina periwinkle is the ONLY ocean creature that can survive in sweet water.

The first U.S. express service founded in 1839 consisted of deliveries by carpet bag.

King Louis IX (1214-1270) was the ONLY French King in the country's entire history that was nursed by his own Mother.

The first church bell in the New World can be seen in Santo Domingo, Dominican Republic.

The first metal lined bathtub was constructed by Adam Thompson of Cincinnati, Ohio, it weighed nearly a ton.

U.S. Supreme Court Justice John A. Campbell (1811-1889) of Alabama is the ONLY member of the court in its entire history whose appointment was requested by fellow jurist.

Paul Deschanel (1856-1922) was the ONLY French president who was not born in France. He was born in Belgium and served as president of France in 1920.

The first aluminum pot of stew pan was made of aluminum by Henry W. Avery of Cleveland, Ohio in 1890.

John Quincy Adams was the first U.S. President to use a middle name.

The Jamaican Railway was the first to be constructed in the British Colonies (1844) and was a private undertaking by two brothers William and David Smith.

Port Royal in Jamaica, W.I. was quoted several times as the hemispheres ONLY existing sunken city, and the "richest and wickedest city on earth". Port Royal was haven for the pirates who roamed the seas and home for the former Buccaneer/ Privateer—Sir Henry Morgan.

Sligoville in St. Catherine, Jamaica was the first free village in that country.

Sean Paul in 2003 became the first reggae/dancehall act to have four singles on The Billboard Charts at the same time.

Paul Hill was executed n September 2003 by lethal injection. He was the first killer of an abortion provider executed in the United States.

Physician Robert Mayer (1814-1878) conceived the first law of thermodynamics but got no credit because he was unable to express it mathematically.

Wilbur and Orville Wright (two bicycle repairmen) made their first powered flight in 1903; Orville ONLY stayed in the air for 12 seconds.

Lance Cpl. Joseph Maglione III, a 22-year-old Marine Corps reservist studying architectural engineering at Drexel University in Philadelphia, Pa was the first American college student to die during the Iraq conflict in 2003.

Lt. Gen. Amer al-Saadi, presidential science adviser to Saddam Hussain, surrendered on April 12, 2003, making the first of the 55 Most Wanted to be captured.

Lucille Ball in 1952 was the first pregnant woman to play a Mother-to-be in a sitcom—but was not allowed to say the word "pregnancy" on TV.

Alfred Kinsey, in 1953, published "Sexual Behavior in the Human Female", the first major U.S. survey on woman's sexual habits.

Paul MacCready became the "father of human flight" during 1977-79 period when his 70-pound Gossamer Condor completed the first sustained, controlled human-powered flight.

Brian Dalton was the first (2003) person in the United States to be successfully prosecuted for child pornography that involved writing, not images.

Snowball was the name given to an albino dolphin, the ONLY one known to exist (Miami Seaquarium, 1962).

In May 1939 Bill Stern the "Colgate Shave Cream" man announced the first remote sports broadcast, on NBC radio.

The first member elected to the Swimming Hall of Fame was Johnny "Tarzan" Weissmuller in 1965; the Hall of Fame is located in Fort Lauderdale, Florida.

The ONLY even prime number is 2.

The TU-144 was the first supersonic transport (SST) plane to fly; it was built by the Russians.

Tarzan, fictional jungle hero (Lord of the Jungle) created in 1914 by Edgar Rice Burroughs "Tarzan of the Apes", first story appeared in All Story magazine in October 1912.

At 10 years of age Elizabeth Taylor made her first appearance in the movie "There's One Born Every Minute" in 1942.

In 1859 Titusville, Pa was the site of the first oil well-drilled by Edwin Drake on August 27th.

Peanut's by Charles Schlz was first published in October 1950 in the U.S.

The ONLY female whose portrait has appeared on U.S. Currency was that of Martha Washington on a One Dollar Silver Certificate in 1891.

Barbara Walters was the first female news broadcaster on network news program. She signed a $5 million, 5-year contract with ABC as the news evening anchorwoman in April 1976.

On September 12, 1910 Alice Wells was sworn in as the first policewoman; she worked for the Los Angeles Police Department (LAPD).

In 1865 "The Yellow Kid" became the first comic strip type cartoon, created by Richard Outcault for NY World.

In January 1997 Ameritech became the first Baby Bell to ask regulators for permission to offer long-distance services.

Rental-car companies can't turn away customers (March 1997) solely because of their age, New York states highest court found, in the first major ruling on a decades-old industry practice.

Fuji Photo made plans in May 1997 to begin manufacturing film in the U.S. for the first time making the Japanese company a more formidable competitor against Eastman Kodak.

The Statue of Liberty was reopened to visitors in August 2004 for the first time since the 2001 terrorist attacks that destroyed the nearby World Trade Center. A new device for screening visitors that blows air through clothing and tests for evidence of explosive particles is a first with this technology.

Pakistani Aafia Siddiqui, the ONLY prominent female figure in al-Qaida, considered by the United States to be a likely "fixer" for the group in the United States and elsewhere.

Marshal Pietro Badoglia, who ordered the use of poison during the reign of fascist dictator Benito Mussolini for Ethiopians, became the first prime minister of postwar Italy and died a national hero.

The Samsung's washing and cleaning technology group is behind a new washing machine that deposits tiny silver particles (the Agt Nano System)—about 1/10,000 the thickness of a human hair—onto clothes to make them bacteria—and odor-free without the use of hot water. The device represents the first (2004) mass-produced application of this type of nano-technology—the science of very small structures—to home appliances.

John Jay was the first Chief Justice of the United States.

Hiram Fong was the son of impoverished Chinese immigrants who became a millionaire businessman and the first Asian American in the U.S. Senate, serving as Hawaii's ONLY Republican Senator for 18 years. He died at age 97 in September 2004.

Life magazine published its first issue in 1936.

In the late nineteenth century the French first discovered a special process of canning foods using heat that would preserve them for a greater length of time.

Some say it was at the Chicago World's Fair—some say it was on Coney Island—that the first frankfurter was introduced.

In 1925 Howard Johnson was the first to establish the mass-market menu. And thus the fast-food chain was born.

Ben Cohen and Jerry Greenfield (Ben & Jerry) opened the doors to their first ice cream parlour in 1978.

In 1954, in Miami, Florida, James McLamore and David Edgeton built the first Burger King Restaurant.

Led by CEO Leonard Rawls, the Hardee's Company opened its first hamburger restaurant in 1961 at the corner of Church Street and Falls Road in Rocky Mount, North Carolina.

In 1950 a man named Robert O'Petersen built the first Jack-in-the-Box restaurant at El Cahon and 63rd streets in SanDiego, California.

The first overseas outlet for KFC was in England. In 1935 the first Kentucky Fried Chicken restaurant opened.

Brothers Dick and Mac McDonald opened the first McDonald's drive-restaurant in 1948 in San Bernardino, California.

Al Lupin opened the first International House of Pancakes in Toluca Lake, California, in 1958.

The name Taco Bell was first officially established in 1962.

In 1969, at the ripe old age of thirty-seven, R. David Thomas left a job at Arthur Treacher's Fish & Chips to open the first Wendy's at 257 E. Broad Street in downtown Columbus, Ohio.

Cheryl Sters was the first female allowed to join the world famous Golden Knights paratrooper/skydiver team from the U.S. Army, Fort Bragg, North Carolina.

The ONLY palaces on U.S. soil that were built for monarchs are in Hawaii.

Fresh Prince (now better known as Will Smith) won a Grammy in 1988 for "Parents Just Don't Understand", the first Grammy for rap.

Dakota, Minnesota & Eastern was seeking to finance a $62 billion freight line form the Midwest to Wyoming (June '97), in a bid to become the first major new U.S. railroad in over 50 years.

On July 16, 1997 the Dow Jones Industrial Average passed the 8,000 point mark for the first time.

IBM said it has become the first company to successfully substitute copper for aluminum in making semiconductors

(September '97), a vital breakthrough in manufacturing faster and more powerful computer chips.

A 12-wheeled contraption named "Chew-Chew" is the first robot to be powered entirely by food.

A type of monkey known as Miss Waldro's red colobus is the first primate species to disappear within the past century.

To save weight, the Airbus A3XX was the first aircraft in 2004 to use carbon fiber composite to connect the wings to the body.

Ford's 2002 Explorer will be the first traditional sport-utility vehicle to use a fully independent rear suspension.

The CIH virus has affected 1 million PC's since it was first triggered on April 26, 1998.

President Reagan, citing concern for the safety of traveling Americans, first imposed the travel ban on Libya in 1981.

The first woman to win Britain's top sports literary prize was Sally Jenkins.

The Dutch Parliament approved a bill on November 28, 2000 to allow euthanasia and physician-assisted suicide, which would make Holland the first country to formally legalize the practice.

Jean-Bertrand Aristide became Haiti's first freely elected leader in 1990, ending nearly 200 years of dictatorship. In November 2000 he was re-elected with an overwhelming 92 percent (92%) of the vote.

On December 25, 1998, Cubans celebrate Christmas for the first time in decades.

Paul Wellstone of Minnesota, a United States Senator made the first-ever visit (December 1, 2000) by a U.S. lawmaker to the deadliest town—Barrancabermeja, Colombia—in all the Americas.

Although roughly 30 million U.S. men suffer from some form of impotence, ONLY a few thousand web surfers watched the world's first (November 2000) Internet broadcast of penile-pump-implant surgery.

A January 1971 centerfold picture in Playboy magazine of Liv Lindland of Norway was the first ever to show pubic hair.

Testosterone was first isolated in 1935, hormone replacement therapy is one of the few areas of medicine where research on men lags behind that on women.

The Oprah Magazine "O" printed 1 million copies for the first issue in April 2000.

Jiang Zemin visited Israel on April 2000, the first Chinese President in history to do so, and when he took a dip in the Dead Sea he may have been the first head of state to go floating.

Ancient Greek physician Dioscorides—the first person known to have used the word "anesthesia"—attributed anesthetic powers to potions made from mandrakes and wine.

The one-mile land speed record is 76303 mph set by Andy Green of OK, in "Thrust ACC" in Black Rock Desert, Nevada, in October 1997. It is the first car to have exceeded the speed of sound.

The Sony Corporation developed the Walkman in 1979, the first model on the market being the TPS-L2.

In 1997, the Israeli Yad Vashen Memorial Museum awarded the late hero Varian Fry its highest accolade, naming him on of the Righteous Among the Nations. He was the first U.S. citizen to receive the tribute.

Popular interest in the principle of teleportation was first kindled in the 1960's by the popular television sci-fi series "Star Trek".

The Hungarian journalist Laszlo Biro created the first ballpoint pen in collaboration with his brother Georg in 1938.

Edwin Land, a U.S. citizen, founder of the Polaroid Corporation in 1937, first demonstrated the Polaroid camera at a meeting of the Optical Society of America in February 1947.

William R. Carey, a project engineer with the U.S. firm Eaton, Yale and Town, was the first to develop the air bag for installation into automobiles and make it a practical safety feature. He registered his patent in 1969.

In 1998, Julie Mills, a student teacher, was kept alive without a pulse for six days by the AB 180 Left Ventricular Assist Drive. She was the fourth person to have the device implanted in the U.S. and the first to survive the procedure.

The first brain cell transplant ever was performed by a team of doctors from the University of Pittsburg Medical Center in Pennsylvania on June 23, 1998.

In March 1997, clinical psychologist Dr. Kimberly Young established the Virtual Clinic, the world's first psychiatric cybercenter for Internet addicts and those with related mental health problems.

George Meegan from Rainham, England walked 19,019 miles from Ushuaia, the Southern tip of South America to Prudhoe

Bay in Northern Alaska, in 2,426 days from January 26, 1977 to September 18, 1983, thus completed the first traverse of the Americas and the Western Hemisphere.

Louis "Satchmo" Armstrong was almost 63 when he had his first U.S. No. 1 hit "Hello Dolly" in 1964.

Louis Eliasberg, the ONLY person known to have ever owned a complete collection of U.S. coins.

Frank Winfield Woolworth opened the first store, The Great Five Cent Store, in Utica, NY, in 1879. In January 1996 the Woolworth Corporation of NY had 8,178 retail stores worldwide. In 1997 they closed all US stores.

Fox's' Independence Day (1996) has grossed $811 million worldwide—the highest box-office gross of any science-fiction film on its first release.

Omar Bradley, US Army Cadet, 1913-14, was the Cadets Centre, was Dwight D. Eisenhower's right man for the Allied invasion of Europe, and was the first chairman of The Joint Chiefs of Staff.

Frank Sinatra holds the record for the longest span of Top 20 Albums in the US and UK. His first US chart entry in the rock era was "In the Wee Small Hours" which entered on May 28, 1955.

The most valuable comic book is a first-issue copy of Action Comics from June 1938, in which Superman made his first appearance.

Invented by Johnston McCulley, Zorro was the first comic strip character to be the subject of a major feature film.

Barbara Walters has interviewed every US president since Richard Nixon, and she made journalistic history when she arranged the first joint interview of President Anwar Sadat of Egypt and Prime Minister Manachem Begin of Israel in November 1977.

The biggest car ever to be produced (22 feet long) for private use was the Bugatti "Royale" type 41, it was first in 1927.

The USAF Lockheed SR-71, a reconnaissance aircraft was the fastest jet ever reaching a speed of 2,193.22 mph; it was first flown in its definitive form in 1964.

Beginning life in the mid-1950's as the SS-6, it was first Soviet inter-continental ballistic missile (ICBM).

Babu Chhiri of Napal completed a stay of 21 hours at the summit of Mt. Everest (29,029 ft.) without the use of bottled oxygen; Babu is the first person to climb the mountain twice in the same season.

L. Frank Baum wrote the fanciful book and 13 sequels—The Wizard of Oz—(turned 100 in year 2000), the film appeared on television for the first time in 1956.

Based on the disappearance of the earliest English Settlers on the Outer Banks, "The Lost Colony" is the US longest-running professional outdoor drama produced by the Roanoke Island Historical Association; the show was launched in 1937 and has closed ONLY once, during World War II.

Wyclef Jean, a member of the Grammy-winning rap group The Fugees and a solo artist, headlined a charity concert at New York City's Carnegie Hall on January 19, 2000, making him the first hip-hop headliner there.

Arrested on drug charges in 1999 and facing a potential life sentence, Ralph Natale became the first sitting mob boss ever to agree to cooperate with the authorities.

Former newspaper cartoonist Tom Darcy, who won the 1970 Pulitzer Prize for editorial cartooning, died Wednesday, December 6, 2000 of emphysema. He was the first in a new wave of editorial cartoonists, who abandoned stylized editorial cartooning.

Though phones sold in the United States are starting to carry notification of radiation levels, Britain was the first country to embark on such a broad precautionary response to health concerns—December 2000.

Honeywell's Web Pad—the first wireless Internet appliance.

Spread betting first hove into view in the mid-1970's, when a British sports bookmaker—betting is legal in Britain—devised an esoteric, high-risk means of gambling on the future of market indices.

When researchers Barry Spletzer and Gary Fischer set out to create the world's first hopping robot, they used grasshoppers as their guides.

John Quincy Adams was the first. In 1824, the son of the second president collected fewer votes than Andrew Jackson, but neither man could muster a majority of the Electoral College.

Fans traveled from as far away as Poland for a chance to meet Paul McCartney (former Beatle) December 13, 2000 at his first book signing—"Paul McCartney: Paintings". McCartney is left-handed.

Frederick August Conrad Muhlenberg was a member of The Continental Congress of the 13 American colonies, and subsequently Speaker of the House of Representatives in 1795.

"Did you like that mama" were the ONLY spoken words in the first talking movie (1927) "The Jazz Singer"—the rest of the "talking" was songs.

Thirty-four experts will present an OAS Commission with the results of the organizations first (December 2000) country-by-country drug study of the America's, known as the Multilateral Evaluation Mechanism, or MEM.

For the first time in history (December 2000), American consumers charged more than $100 billion to their major credit cards during the holiday season.

Appointed in 1981 by President Reagan, Sandra Day O'Connor was an Arizona State Legislator and State Appeals Court Judge before taking her seat as the first woman on the U.S. Supreme Court.

University of Utah biologist Baldomero Olivera, first isolated the venom component of the Conus magos snail that became ziconotide. Ziconotide is 1,000 times more potent than morphine.

Oldsmobile grew steadily over the years and in 1977 became the first GM division outside Chevrolet to sell more than 1 million cars.

In 1999, for the first time in decades, Americans' consumption of carbonated soft drinks actually declined.

In 1856 the White House received its first Christmas Tree.

Sean Connery, Hollywood's first James Bond, sang a love song in the cult classic "Darby O'Gill and the Little People".

The star of Hollywood's first western was Buffalo Bill Cody.

Statistics show that ONLY one quarter of the records released in any given year make money and ONLY 17 new artists a year ever break into the Top 40.

John Milton's epic "Paradise Lost" sold ONLY 40 copies on its first printing.

Edgar Allan Poe sold his first book for twelve cents (12cts).

The world's first "perfect book"—"Horace"—was published in 1744 ONLY after six proofreaders read every page 500 time.

Dr. Lea De Forest, the father of radio, his vacuum tubes made it possible for the first radio broadcast in 1910, a recording of Caruso.

Fred Morrison invented Frisbee, and in 1957 the first batch was produced in California.

The Greeks and Chinese first started speculating in sugar and then it was gradually replaced by honey.

The first thing a Martian would notice about Earth is not earth but water. This miraculous combination of elements is the basis for all terrestrial life.

The first rash of UFO sightings started in the U.S. in 1896—just about the time inventors were pushing ahead with plans for the first flying machines.

Dinosaur hunting is booming. Nearly 300 types have been named since the first dinosaur fossils were discovered in the 19th century.

The earthquakes about a million times a year, ONLY five out of the million actually kill people or damage property.

British mountaineer Douglas Haston, one of the two men who were first to scale Mount Everest by the southwest face in 1976, was swept to his death by an avalanche while skiing in the Alps in January 1977.

The first zip fastener was invented by Whitcomb L. Judson of Chicago in 1891.

ONLY 1 percent (1%) of all deaths in Ontario, Canada, occurs in the home.

Instant coffee was introduced n 1934 but ONLY began to be produced in quantity in 1956.

ONLY one percent (1%) of all patents ever become successful products.

A suspicious ships captain and wireless telegraphy brought the arrest of American-born murderer Hawley Harvey Cripper. In the first (August 1915) such use of wireless telegraphy, the captain wired Scotland Yard and the couple were arrested when the ship docked.

ONLY one in 100 computer crimes is ever detected, much less successfully prosecuted.

Men may be stronger physically, but that's about the ONLY biological advantage nature has given them.

In Catholic Italy, there's ONLY one divorce for every 26 marriages.

The first electron microscope in North America was built at the University of Toronto by Eli Burton.

The first solid-state computer was developed at Ferranti Electric Ltd. just after World War II by Dr. Arthur Porter.

Francois Vautier stunned the French medical world in 1631 when he became the first to use antimony powder in all his cures.

On January 26, 1935 canned beer is first sold.

ONLY spirits made from the blue agaves (a desert plant descended for the lily) plant are tequila.

In June 2001 the first Euro-Hooters opened in Paris.

Out of this era of Mutually Assured Destruction (MAD) came the Single Integrated Operations Plan—a streamlined etched, etched-in-stone launch protocol. The code word for the first SIOP was Dropkick.

First bred in Germany, Rottweilers—big powerful animals often used as guard dogs—have surpassed pit bulls as the deadliest breed of canines in the United States.

ONLY your doctor can weigh the risks versus the benefits of any prescription drug.

ONLY five percent (5%) of all species of mammal are monogamous.

The AT&T Building in NYC, New York was the first postmodern building that became memorable to the public—1982.

In 1960 the world's first weather satellite, TIROS was launched.

In 1971 the first orbital space station was established.

In 1973 Skylab 2, became the U.S. first orbital space station.

The first reusable crewed spacecraft, the space shuttle Columbia of the U.S. was launched on April 12, 1981.

In 1913 the first crossword puzzle was published.

The North Carolina State Supreme Court threw out the murder conviction of drunken driver Thomas R. Jones (December 2000), the case was believed to be the first in the U.S in which prosecutors sought the death penalty in a driving-while-impaired case.

In 1893 the Jehovah's Witnesses first major convention was held in Chicago, Illinois, it was attended by 300 people and 70 new ones to be baptized.

The United Nations (UN) adopted the first major overhaul of its financing in more than two decades (December 23, 2000), cutting U.S. payments to the world body and shifting most of the financial burden to developing countries that have experienced economic improvement.

Researchers everywhere involved in a cure for cancer still seek Henrietta Locks cells, the first human cells available for cancer experimentation.

The Prophet Mohammad had no sons and no obvious successor. The minority Shiite sect believes Muhammad's Son-in-law, Ali, to be the first true successor.

Johannes Brahms, the famed German composer took nearly 20 years to complete his first symphony.

American Edmund Pope became the first (December 2000) American convicted of espionage in Russia in 40 years.

Spindletop Hill in Beaumont, Texas was the first Texas oil well.

Cigarettes are the ONLY legal product that, when used as directed, cause death.

Cardiomyopathy is a condition in which the muscle of the heart is abnormal in the absence of an apparent cause. It was first recognized in the late 1950s.

For the first time, concrete was used in a sculptural way to create a fluid structure in the building of the Church of Notre-Dame-du-Haut, Ronchamp, Vorges, France—1955.

The Jesus-in-Japan theory first emerged in the 1930's when researchers claimed to have found a "will of Christ"—the original of which was lost during World War II—indicating that Jesus was buried in Shingo, Japan.

The Canadian government has chosen Prairie Plant Systems of Saskatoon to provide the country with its first (December 2000) legal supply of marijuana for medical and research purposes.

The FBI for the first time (December 2000) placed a child pornography suspect—Eric Franklin Rosser—on its Ten Most Wanted Fugitives.

Lucille Ball appeared with her baby son Desidario Arnaz IV on the cover of the first issue of TV Guide (April 3-9, 1953).

Simon Bernard performed the first operation for appendicitis in the United States in 1888.

John Birch is considered to have been the first American killed by the Communists after World War II.

On January 23, 1946 J.T. Callahan became the first U.S. Navy Chaplain to be awarded the Medal of Honour.

The novel "The Cardinal's Mistress" written by Benito Mussolini in 1909 was the ONLY novel the Italian Dictator wrote.

Montgomery Ward Inc. began in 1872. Ward pioneered mail-order catalogues when it came out with a single sheet of dry-good items for sale. It was the first U.S. Mail-order house to sell general merchandise. Montgomery Ward filed for bankruptcy in December 2000.

Avant, a cosmetic company in Kyoto, Japan has introduced what it calls the world's first body-washing machine, the Sante Lubian 999, in the year 2000.

The 1952 recording of "It Wasn't God Who Made Honky Tonk Angels" by Kitty Wells was the first No 1 country hit by a female singer.

The first ice hotel built on the North American continent was built in Quebec, Canada and cost $100 per night.

Princess Margaret, sister of Queen Elizabeth II of Great Britain became the first inner circle royal divorce—from Lord Snowden—since Henry VIII.

Sophia Loren, 1960 Italian film "Two Women" and Roberto Benigni 1997, for "Life is Beautiful" are the ONLY two foreign-language films to be awarded the Oscar.

James Buchanan was the ONLY bachelor United States President.

Intel invented the microprocessor in 1971, and the first video arcade game, Pong, arrived a year later.

Walter Brennan is the ONLY actor to win the Academy Award for best supporting actor 3 times:

Come and Get It (1936), Kentucky (1938), The Westerner (1940).

Don Brown was the first person to cross the Golden Gate Bridge when it opened May 27, 1937.

The Bulova Watch Company was the sponsor of the first television commercial July 1, 1941, at a cost of ONLY $9.00.

Hattie Caraway (Ophelia Wyatt) was the first woman elected to the U.S. Senate on January 11, 1932.

Dr. John S. Pemberton of Atlanta, Georgia invented Coca-Cola in 1886; Coca Cola was first sold at Jacobs Pharmacy May 8, 1886.

John Dillinger was America's first Public Enemy Number One; Bank robber (1902-1934) killed in Chicago by FBI men.

Dopey, one of The Seven Dwarfs, is the ONLY one without a beard.

America's first ace (5 kills) pilot was Lt. Douglas Campbell on May 31, 1918.

The Flamingo Hotel in Las Vegas was the first hotel built on the famous Las Vegas Strip and cost ONLY $6 million in 1906.

"Humorous Phases of Funny Phases" (1906), made by Thomas Edison with drawings by James Stourt Blackkton was the first cartoon on film.

Sarah Huges, U.S. District Judge who swore in Lyndon Johnson the day John F. Kennedy was assassinated, is the ONLY woman ever to administer the presidential oath.

The "U.S.S. Kearsarge" is the ONLY battleship not named after a state.

The Lincoln Memorial first appeared on the reverse side of the Lincoln penny (cent) in 1959.

Military Bandsmen in Saudi Arabia are the ONLY inhabitants among a population of 6,500,000 permitted to play any type of music.

The sulphur sponge is the ONLY animal life that can dissolve sea shells into the original calcium from which they were formed.

The first inflated money, gold discs minted in Germany over 2,000 years ago as coins without inscriptions indicating their value, increased in worth when the mint spread the rumor they had been found at the end of the rainbow.

The ONLY disinfectant available when an epidemic of small pox swept the town of Oglethorpe, Georgia in 1855 was garlands of onions.

The first Nebula Award (given annually by Science Fiction Writers of America) was given to Frank Herbert for "Dune" in 1965.

Judy Neuffer was the U.S. Navy's first female pilot.

The "U.S.S. Pennsylvania" was the first U.S. Navy cruiser on which an airplane landed—January 18, 1911.

Fred Waring's orchestra "The Pennsylvanians" was the first band ever to appear on TV.

Franklin Delano Roosevelt is the ONLY United States President to be elected for four terms: 1932, 1936, 1940, 1944.

Bucks County, Pennsylvania Congressman Jim Greenwood has been named (January 2001) Chair of the Oversight and Investigations Subcommittee (under the George W. Bush, Sr. administration). He's the first chairman form Bucks since 1928. Greenwood resigned form being a Congressman in August 2004.

First introduced in 1899, Pall Mall became the first king-size cigarette in 1839. It's popularity peaked in the 1960's when it was the nation's top-selling brand.

Researchers have created (October 2000) the world's first genetically modified primate—a baby rhesus monkey with jelly-fish DNA that glows green in the dark.

The Supremes were ONLY paid $15 per week for their first gigs as the Primettes. Between 1964 and 1968 ONLY the Beatles and Elvis Presley sold more records.

Judge Ronnie White of Missouri was the first judicial nominee since conservative jurist Robert Bork in 1987 to suffer defeat on the floor of the U.S. Senate.

Ernest Hemingway ONLY wrote one play—"The Fifth Column".

Theodore Roosevelt in 1901 became the ONLY U.S. President not sworn in with his hand on the Bible. In 1905 the first telephone lines were installed at the Capitol for the inauguration.

Warren G. Harding became the first President in 1925 to ride to and from his inauguration in a car.

In 1925 Calvin Coolidge was the first U.S. President to broadcast his inauguration nationally by radio.

Franklin D. Roosevelt in 1907 became the first President inaugurated on January 20th due to the 20th Amendment.

In 1949 Harry S. Truman became the first President to have a televised inaugural ceremony.

In 1965 Lyndon B. Johnson used a bullet-proof closed limousine for the first time.

In 1974 Gerald R. Ford became the first unelected Vice President—Spiro T. Agnew had resigned in 1973—to become President of the United States.

Jimmy Carter in 1977 was the first President to walk from the Capitol to the White House with his family after the inaugural ceremony. It was the first time an outgoing President (Ford) left the Capitol by helicopter.

Ronald Reagan had his first inaugural ceremony in 1981 on the west front of the Capitol. In 1985 for the first time the swearing-in took place in the Capitol Rotunda.

In 1865 in Abraham Lincoln's inaugural parade, Black Americans were able to participate for the first time.

Lt. Cmdr. Michael S. Speicher, whose jet was hit on the first night of the Gulf War in 1991, is the ONLY American lost in Iraqi territory who has not been accounted for. Speicher was declared Killed in Action (KIA). In January 2001 the Navy changed his KIA to Missing in Action (MIA). This is the first time that the

Navy have ever changed a KIA status; not in the Civil War, WWI, WWII or in VietNam.

Swiss-born actress Ursula Andress rose to stardom when she emerged from the sea wearing a cotton bikini in the 1962 movie "Dr. No", the first 007 movie.

Piotr Chmielinski, a Herndon, Va., environmental consultant, is the ONLY person to have traveled the entire navigable length of the Amazon by boat.

The first Tuesday after the first Monday in November is Election Day.

Euclid Ave. and East 105th street in Cleveland, Ohio, intersection where the first traffic light in the U.S. was installed—August 5, 1914.

George W. Bush, who was inaugurated Saturday January 20, 2001, is a firm death penalty supporter: 152 inmates were put to death during his tenure as Texas Governor; and ONLY once during nearly six years in office did he ever use his power to stop an execution.

Pope John Paul II was the fist Pope with two names; he did this in remembrance of his predecessors.

Chiquita was the first banana company that sold bananas by the brand name.

Chuck Yeager's X-1 (X is for experimental), was the first supersonic airplane.

The Precept by GM, is the ONLY vehicle to achieve the mileage (80 miles per gallon) anticipated by the Partnership for a New

Generation Vehicle program, a joint research project undertaken by several American auto companies and the U.S. government.

The Office of Strategic Services (OSS) looked to the Sears & Roebuck model of shopping, creating a catalogue of latest gear for the well equipped spy. The first catalogue was issued in July 1944.

On October 15, 1997, Andy Green became the first person to officially break the sound barrier on land as he piloted the Thrust SSC jet-powered car to more than 763 mph in less than a minute.

Sprint PCS started selling (December 2001) the first cell phone and watch combo (address book, speaker-phone, and head phone jack) available in the United States.

Voyetra Turtle Beach's Audio Station remote is the first to also control the digital jukebox on your PC to play back digital music files.

James Bond's (007) first car was a Bentley.

In 1883 the term lesbian is first used to describe a homosexual woman.

In 1921 sixteen-year-old Margaret Gorman wins the first Miss America contest, despite having measurements of ONLY 30-25-32.

In 1974 the world's first penile implant is successfully performed—on a 70-year-old Russian.

In 1999 the first virtual sex program is marketed.

Kawasaki Prairie 4X4 is the first all-terrain vehicle (ATV) with a V-twin engine, which means it gets twice as many power strokes as a single cylinder.

George W. Bush on January 20, 2001 became the first President to follow his father into the White House since John Quincy Adams in 1824 and it was the first time since Joseph P. Kennedy saw John F. Kennedy take the oath of office in 1961 that a father witnessed his son being sworn in to the White House.

Ukuleles were first crafted in Hawaii in 1879 by Portuguese immigrants, and their plinking sound—the instrument's name means "jumping flea"—has been synonymous with the islands ever since.

ONLY hummingbirds can fly backwards.

In Peru, South America, people who speak Quechua, the ONLY language of the Inca.

Miramax Films became the first (January 2001) major studio to release a feature movie ("Guinevere") over the Internet as Hollywood mobilizes to head off the "Napsterization" of motion pictures.

Tiny Tim's ONLY #1 top 40 tune was "Tip Toe Through The Tulips".

Franklin Delano Roosevelt never took an unaided step after his polio attack in 1921. ONLY two photographs of him in a wheelchair exist.

In 1980 the first genetically modified mouse was created by inserting a new gene into the mouse bone-marrow cells and then putting those cells into a living animal.

In 1874 the first traveler's cheques (check) are sold by Thomas Cook.

The Statler Co. becomes the first successful hotel chain, originating in Buffalo, New York in 1908.

Hertz developed the first (1925) national rental-car company, a "Drive-Ur-Self-System".

In 1950 Diners' Club becomes the first universal credit card.

In 1981 American Airlines launches the first frequent-flyer program: AAdvantage.

Jesuit theologian Avery Dulles of Fordham University, the son of former Secretary of State John Foster Dulles, is the first U.S. theologian to be named a cardinal—January 2001.

During the first Bush administration Ann Veneman was the highest ranking woman to serve in the U.S. Department of Agriculture, in 2001 she became the first woman to run it.

China signed a deal with a German consortium on January 23, 2001 to build the world's first commercial train to float on magnetic fields.

Legendary recording artist Ray Charles sang "America the Beautiful," followed by "The National Anthem" sung by the Backstreet Boys at the Super Bowl Game XXXV. It will mark the first time the two songs will be performed prior to the start of the game, January 28, 2001. Ray Charles died in 2004.

Princeton's Board of Trustees (January 27, 2001) pledged that come September 2001 no undergraduate receiving financial aid will have to take out loans to pay for school; it's the first of its kind at a university.

Sgt. Clyde Thompson of Atlanta, Ga. was the first enlisted Marine awarded the Medal of Honor during World War II.

Bats are the ONLY true mammals that have mastered flight.

President George W. Bush Jr. joined Senate Democrats at their private retreat on February 1, 2001, it was the first time a sitting Republican President joined opposition lawmakers at a congressional retreat.

One of the largest, loudest and most brightly coloured monkeys in Africa has vanished without a trace. Called Miss Waldron's red colobus, it lived in Ghana and the Ivory Coast. Scientists are especially worried, because it's the first primate to disappear in 300 years.

In the 130-year history of Ringling Bros. Barnum & Bailey Circus ONLY one worker has been killed by an animal.

Gallaudet University, Washington, D.C., is the ONLY college for the deaf in the United States as of year 2003.

In January 2001 (George W. Bush Jr. is President) the ONLY Black Republican in the U.S. Congress was J.C. Watts from Oklahoma. Watts resigned from Congress in 2002.

On February 6, 2001 Ronald Reagan, the 40th President celebrated his 90th birthday, thus become one of ONLY three U.S. Presidents to live 90 or more years. The others were John Adams and Herbert Hoover. Ronald Reagan died on June 5, 2004.

Gerald Ford was the first to sense that the presidency could be merchandised. Ford understood that the president was, besides being commander-in-chief and all of that, the U.S. No.1 celebrity.

For the first time (February 2001), doctors found a treatment that cuts the death rate from sepsis (colloquially known as blood poisoning, can occur in response to almost any bacterial infection).

Abraham "Abe" D. Beame, the diminutive accountant who served as the 104th mayor of New York City, died on February 10, 2001, Beame was the city's first Jewish mayor.

The first U.S. President to attend a World Series game was Woodrow Wilson. He saw the Phillies beat the Red Sox in the 1915 Series opener.

Alaska is the ONLY U.S. State without termites.

For the first time ever (February 2001), prolific horror scribe Stephen King has penned a screenplay based on another writer's book.

Uruguayan President Jorge Batlle became (February 2001) the first head of state in the region—and one of the few anywhere—to call for the decriminalization of illicit drugs.

A spacecraft successfully completed history's first landing on an asteroid (EROS) about 196 million miles from earth—February 12, 2001. It was the first time an American craft had made an initial unmanned landing on an outer space body.

At first Sesame Street's Big Bird was ONLY on for two minutes. By the second, he was getting more air time. Caroll Spinney, born December 26, 1933 has been the human inside Big Bird since 1969.

Solitary reggae singer and Gulf War veteran Orville "Shaggy" Richard Burcel (a born Jamaican) passed Jennifer Lopez

(February 1, 2001), making him the first reggae artist ever to top the pop charts since Shabba Ranks in 1991.

The first clinical trial (February 2001) to look at strokes and hormone replacement therapy (HRT) shows no increase or decrease—at least in post-menopausal women with heart disease.

Zenith's Internet TV 27-inch is the world's first TV with Internet and e-mail access built in.

The world's first television with a built-in disc-based recorder; Konka's VD 278.

Brian Hubert, a graduate from MIT, has developed the world's first universal nano-assembly machine, capable of picking up and assembling virtually any type of material, several thousand atoms at a time.

Under rules announced by President George Bush Sr. on August 26, 1992 Iraqi's planes were banned from the skies south of the 33rd parallel and north of the 36th. December 17, 1992, marked the first shooting, when a Southern Watch F-16 shot down an Iraqi MIG.

Betty Ray Rotenberg, the first woman to earn a degree in architecture from the University of Pennsylvania, died Tuesday, February 13, 2001 at the age of 87.

On February 17, 2001, North and South Korea exchanged lists of 100 people from each side to participate in family reunions for the first time since the Korean War in the early 1950's.

Bill Clinton in 2001 joined George Bush, Ronald Reagan, Jimmy Carter and Gerald Ford as a member of a very exclusive club. There have been five living former presidents ONLY twice before: When Clinton took office in 1993 (Bush, Reagan, Carter, Ford and Nixon, who died in 1994) and in 1861 (James Buchanan, Franklin Pierce, Millard Fillmore, John Tyler and Martin Van Buren).

Belgian Finance Minister Didier Reynders was the first "euro group" chairman form a non-Group of Seven nation to attend a G7 gathering in February 2001. The meeting also marked the first time a euro group official helped draft the final statement.

The Volkswagen Beetle, designed by Ferdinand Porsche in 1935, was the first car manufactured to be fuel efficient.

The first tattoo shop was opened in New York City in 1846 by Martin Hildebrandt.

America's first hot dogs arrived here in 1852 inspired by butchers in Frankfurt, Germany who thought it was time for a thinner sausage.

"Steamboat Willie", first shown in 1928, was America's first animated cartoon with sound.

Ronald Reagan was the first president with an ex-wife. He was divorced from Jane Wyman in 1940 and married Nancy Davis 12 years later.

UNICEF released a first ever table of "Safest Nations for Children" (February 2001). It surveyed 26 countries on the basis of youth injury. Countries declared "safest" are Sweden, the U.K., Netherlands, and Norway.

America's trade deficit with the rest of the world surged to a record $369.7 billion in the year 2000, even though U.S. exports topped $1 trillion for the first time.

A lawsuit was filed Wednesday February 26, 2001 (Mass. Double-dipping from dead smokers) on behalf of the estate of May Watkins. This lawsuit appears to be the first that challenges a system in place in states nationwide.

There have been several rape convictions at both the Yugoslav tribunal and another U.N. court on the Rwandan genocide. The Foca case (February 2001) was the first international war crimes trial to focus on sexual crimes.

Reggae's first Grammy Award was won in 1985 by Black Uhuru for the seminal album "Anthem". The Grammy is viewed around the world as a symbol of major success.

Russia's first new nuclear power plant since the Soviet era was launched on February 23, 2001.

On February 23, 2001 Argentina said that they had reached a deal with Britain to allow planes and boats of Argentine origin to travel to the Falkland Islands for the first time since the two countries 1982 war over the island's sovereignty.

The U.S.S. Ronald Reagan, the Navy's 10th nuclear-powered aircraft carrier, is the first carrier ever named for a living former President. The aircraft carrier was christened by Nancy Reagan in March 2001.

U.S. Steel, now part of USX Corp. was the United States' first and biggest steel company. It was founded from industrialist Andrew Carnegie's Carnegie Steel Co. on February 25, 1901.

Among the 50 states, ONLY Texas consumes more energy—measured by its total use of electricity, natural gas and oil—than California, the nation's most populous state.

Katherine Blodgett was the first woman hired as a research scientist by General Electric. Twenty-years later she was awarded a patent for her invention of nonreflecting "invisible" glass", used to this day in eyeglasses, picture frames, telescopes, cameras and microscopes.

Harriet Irwin's space-efficient hexagonal house still stands in her home town of Charlotte, N.C. Not ONLY was she the first woman to patent a house design (in 1898), but she built it herself.

Margaret Knight was the first woman to fight and win a patent suit when a man tried to steal her first patent claiming women didn't have the mechanical knowledge to invent such a complex machine.

Stephanie Kwoleck invented Kevlar in 1966 while working as one of the very few female chemists at DuPont. Kevlar is a lightweight substance five times stronger than steel. First marketed in 1971, it is used in bulletproof vests, radial tyres (tires), tennis rackets, brake pads, helmets and sails.

Sybilla Masters was awarded a patent in her husband's name by the English courts in 1715 for her method of making cornmeal from maize. She often is called the first woman inventor in the American colonies.

Margaret Corbin was the first known woman to serve in the Revolutionary War and was awarded the first pension.

The first and ONLY woman to receive the Medal of Honor was Dr. Mary E. Walker, a contract surgeon during the Civil War.

Ann Leah was the first woman to receive The Purple Heart after she was wounded while serving at Hickham Field during the Japanese attack on Pearl Harbor.

A member of the Army Nurse Corps, Lt. Cordelia E. Cook, was the first woman to receive the Bronze Star.

On Tuesday the 13th, 1781 Brit Sir William Herschel cast the first eager eye on Uranus.

The electrocution chair has made blazing headlines, although it's used in ONLY 22 percent (22%) of American executions.

The first Sea-Air-Land (SEAL) teams date back to 1943, when they were known as Naval Construction Battalions.

Since the first White Castle Slyder was opened in Wichita, Kansas in 1921, weight-unconscious Americans have sucked down 12 billion Slydes (or rat burgers, as they're sometimes called), enough to carpet 10,000 football fields.

Mary Lyon founded the first women's college in the United States in 1837, Mount Holyoke College, which still operates as a liberal arts college for women in South Hadley, Massachusetts.

Junko Tabei was the first women to reach the summit of Mt. Everest.

Alia Wells became the first policewoman in the U.S. in 1910.

Julia Child became the first woman designated a full-fledged chef in 1958.

Muriel Siebert was the first woman to own a seat on the New York Stock Exchange in 1967. She was also the first-ever U.S. discount broker and the first woman to serve as Superintendent of Banks for the State of New York.

In March 2001, the United States gave an American shipping company permission to transport products for U.S. producers under a new law allowing American food sales to Cuba for the first time in 40 years.

Mary Baker Eddy was the first and ONLY American woman to found a lasting American-based religion when she began the Church of Christ (Scientist) in 1839.

The national census allowed Americans for the first time to check off more than one race in the year 2000.

ONLY 25.4 percent (25.4%) of adults met government recommendations for physical activity in 1998—virtually unchanged from the beginning of the decade.

In 1870 Ada H. Kepley of Illinois graduated from the Union College of Law in Chicago, making her the first woman lawyer to graduate from law school.

The Directors Guild of America (DGA), often considered the predictor of the upcoming Oscar race, has erred ONLY four times in its 53 year history.

Panavision ONLY rents their cameras and equipment.

"One Flew Over the Cuckoo's Nest" and "Silence of the Lambs" won all four major Oscars (Best Actor, Actress Director and Film. The ONLY other film to sweep was "It Happened One Night" (1934), which won as Best Film and earned Oscars for Clark Gable, Claudette Colbert, director Frank Capra and screenwriter Robert Riskin.

Gertrude Belle Elion, a pharmacologist, was the first woman admitted to the National Inventors Hall of Fame in 1988. She invented the leukemia-fighting drug 6-mercaptopurine and drugs that facilitated kidney transplants.

Winding up a two-week tour (March 12, 2001) of Southern Mexico, the Zapatista leaders became the first rebel group to openly ride in the city since revolutionary leaders Pancho Villa and Emiliano Zapata—the rebels' namesake—did it in 1914.

Annie Moore was the first immigrant to pass through Ellis Island. In 1892, at the age of 15, she came from County Cork, Ireland.

Queen Isabella of Spain became the first woman to appear on a U.S. postage stamp in 1893.

Spanish American War nurse Clara Maass was the first military woman to be memorialized on a U.S. postage stamp.

Inhabitants of Connecticut accounted for one in every six reported cases of Lyme desease in 1999. Lyme was first tracked nationally ONLY 15 years (1991) ago.

Gregory XII was the first Pope to resign.

Delaware County's tiny borough of Millbourne is the first municipality in Pennsylvania with an Asian majority, according to the 2000 U.S. Census Bureau figures.

The Berry Amendment requires the Pentagon to buy ONLY American-made clothing for U.S. troops.

Anna Lelkes became the first official female member of the Vienna Philharmonic in 1997 after the orchestra voted to end its all-male policy. She plays the harp.

Willem Pretorius' farm would be the first to be expropriated under South Africa's 2001 program to redistribute land to Blacks.

In 1963 Valentina Vladimirovna Tereshkova, a Russian cosmonaut, became the first woman in space.

In 1960, Jerrie Cobb was the first woman in the U.S. to undergo astronaut testing.

In 1983 Sally Kristen Ride became the first U.S. woman in space when she participated in a mission from June 18th to the 24th.

Eileen Marie Collins was the first female space shuttle pilot. In 1995 she piloted the space shuttle Discovery on a mission to rendezvous with the Russian Space Station Mir. She became the first female astronaut to command a space shuttle mission four years later.

Scandinavia is a little more connected these days. The summer of 2000 marked the opening of The Oresund Fixed Link, the first tie between Sweden and Denmark since the ice age sundered the countries about 7,000 years ago.

Rome was the first city in the world to reach a population of one million by A.D. 1.

Rosika Schwimmer was the world's first woman ambassador. She was appointed in 1918 to be Hungarian Ambassador to Switzerland.

In 1949, Eugenia Anderson was named Ambassador to Denmark, the first U.S. woman ambassador.

Barbara Jo Rubin became the first woman jockey to win a race in North America. She did it in 1969 aboard Cohesian at Charlestown Race Course in West Virginia.

Few people know that the term "hot dog" was created ONLY after "beef sphincters" scored poorly in focus-group testing.

Brooklyn's 5'2" Kid Twist turned canary in 1940 and provided Brooklyn's district attorney with the first in-depth information about La Nostra's national syndicate.

Salvatore "Sammy the Bull" Gravano was the world's first incognito with a press agent.

Yap's Qian Fish Farm, Singapore, is the world's first ornamental fish farm to trade shares on a public exchange.

Marie Skladowska Curie won the Nobel Prize for physics in 1900 and again for chemistry in 1911, thus becoming the first person to win two Nobel Prizes.

In March 2001 James "Whitey" Bulger of Boston, Mass., was the ONLY senior citizen on the FBI's 10 Most Wanted List.

Joan Crawford was the first guest on "The Tonight Show" with Johnny Carson when it deputed on October 1, 1962.

Mia Farrow appeared on the cover of the first People magazine in 1974.

President Theodore Roosevelt was the first president to receive The Medal of Honor.

Three countries elected their first female prime minister in the 20th century: Golda Meir of Israel, 1969-1974, Indira Gandhi of India became prime minister in 1966; Margaret "Iron Lady" Thatcher of England, who served from 1979-1990.

In 1969 Evelyn Berezin founder Redactron, the first company devoted exclusively to word processors. Though the company was very small, it was the second largest word-processing manufacturer in the world, after IBM.

Ada Byron Lovelace got the idea that engines could calculate Bernoulli numbers and is regarded as the first computer program. In 1979 the U.S. Dept. of Defense named a computer language "Ada" in her honour.

President Jacques Chirac refused to testify before a judge investigating corruptions. It was the first time in the history of France's Fifth Republic that an investigating magistrate has summoned a president, and Chirac clearly saw it as a political maneuver.

Converse first started making it's All Star shoe in 1917, an American standard that in 80 years has changed ONLY in subtle ways.

Anne-Marie Thus and Helene Faasen of Amsterdam, Netherlands, became, on April 1, 2001, the world's first lesbians to be officially married, under legislation recognizing same-sex marriages with full and equal rights. ONLY Dutch nationals or resident foreigners living with a Dutch partner will be eligible for same-sex marriages.

America's first canine hero: Stubby, a bull terrier who served with the 102nd Infantry, was awarded a Victory Medal for his valor during World War I.

Calvin Coolidge died in 1933 leaving a will with ONLY one sentence leaving everything to his wife.

Persian Gulf War veteran, Sgt. Timothy McVeigh died by lethal injection on June 11, 2001 in Terre Haute, Ind. It was the first federal execution since March 1963.

Ralph Natale was the first sitting American Mafia Boss to agree to testify for the prosecution in April 2001. He was a major trophy for law enforcement, particularly the Philadelphia office of the FBI.

The Jerry Springer Show is the first talk show to upstage 'Oprah', hosted by Oprah Winfrey.

California tycoon Dennis Tito paid up to $20 million for a one week tour of Space Station Alpha. Escorted by the Russian Cosmonauts, he was the first person in the world to buy his way into space as a tourist. May 2001.

Former President Joseph Estrada of the Philippines turned himself in on April 16, 2001 after a warrant was issued for his arrest. It was the first time the Philippines issued an arrest warrant for a president.

The Rutland (Vt.) Herald, circulation 22,000 won its first Pulitzer for David Moats' editorials supporting civil unions for gay couples. Civil unions eventually became state law.

The first product to have a bar code was Wrigley's gum.

In a deck of cards the king of hearts is the ONLY king without a mustache.

The first CD pressed in the United States was Bruce Springsteen's "Born in the USA".

The first owner of the Marlboro Company died of lung cancer.

Betsy Ross is the ONLY real person to ever have been the head on a Pez dispenser.

Richard Milhouse Nixon was the first U.S. President whose name contains all the letters from the word "criminal". The second was William Jefferson Clinton.

George W. Bush is the first U.S. President to father twins (Jenna and Barbara).

Pope John Paul II visited Greece on May 4, 2001, the first Pope to visit Greece in nearly 13 centuries.

The first steam engine was based on a pressure cooker.

Shirley M. Calwell Tilghman, a member of the Princeton University faculty and an architect of the national effort to map the human genome, was elected on May 5, 2001 to become the first female president of the University.

Norway's Radio Tango became the world's first radio channel to broadcast daily nude weather forecasts during its morning show in May of 2001.

Everardo Arturo Paez Martinex, known as "El Kitti," was the first accused criminal extradited from Mexico to the U.S. to face charges related to massive drug distribution and money laundering in May of 2001.

The world's first contraceptive patch is as safe and effective as the pill, and easier to remember to use, research suggests.

A 28 year-old construction worker James Hutton from Keizer, Oregon, was credited with bowling just the fifth perfect 900 series in the 106-year (2001) history of the sports national governing body, thus becoming the first Mexican-American to accomplish the feat.

George Washington was the ONLY president to die in the 18th century.

The first machines for the manufacturing of glass marbles were introduced in Germany and the U.S. in 1890.

Acting Gov. Jane Swift of Massachusett, was the first woman in U.S. history to give birth while serving as governor. She gave birth by Caesarean section to twins May 15, 2001.

In May 2001 fourteen women became the first female cadets at Virginia Military Institute (VMI) to finish four years at the previously all-male university.

Maurice Ashley—a Jamaican—is the world's first and ONLY black grandmaster of chess. ONLY 500 others (as of May 2001) worldwide hold the rank.

Comedian, actor and writer George Carlin was the first host of "Saturday Night Live".

Trotsky was a leader in the Russian Bolshevik Revolution and was second ONLY to Lenin. After Lenin's death Trotsky clashed with Stalin, was expelled from the Communist Party, and was later murdered.

The Caribbean, or West Indian, monk seal was the first seal spotted by Columbus in the New World. The last recorded Caribbean monk seal was seen in 1952.

Horses (animal) and horseradish (root) are connected in name ONLY. Horseradish, a member of the mustard family, gets its bite from isothicyanate, fiery oil released when the root is grated or ground.

ONLY female mosquitoes prey on mammals. They need a blood feeding every three or four days to get the protein necessary for egg production.

The first scientific experiment (May 2001) to investigate a possible link between cramped seating on long-hour flights and potentially deadly blood clots, indicates most passengers can sit back and relax.

Trucking is virtually the ONLY industry in the United States that cannot today recruit students out of high school.

Two Americans (May 2001) became the first blind climbers Erik Wiehenmayer of Golden, Colorado, and Sherman Bull, 64, a physician from New Canaan, Connecticut, were the oldest climbers to reach the summit of Mount Everest.

Rep. David Wu, a Democrat from Oregon, was the ONLY Chinese-American ever elected to the U.S. Congress—Year 2002.

Canh Oxelson is the world's first Tiger Woods impersonator. Oxelson, a 6'2", 29 year-0ld Harvard graduate (Year 2001) and a 20 handicapper was born to a Vietnamese mother and an African-American father.

The funkiest condom is Night Light, the first glow-in-the-dark condom cleared for marketing by the FDA.

The change in command brought an end the first period in 50 years (June 2001) in which Republicans held control of the White House and both houses of Congress. It also marked the first time in history when (Senator James Jeffords of Vermont left the Republicans to be independent) when that one party ceded power to another without an intervening election.

The first annual World Stunt Awards was taped for TV Broadcast on May 20, 2001 in Santa Monica, California. Stunt pros worldwide voted for the awards.

On Tuesday September 11, 2001 the twin towers of the World Trade Center in New York and the Pentagon were bombed by hijacked airplanes. It was the first time since D-Day (1944) in WWII that all baseball games in the U.S. were cancelled.

The alarm clock snooze button set for 9 minutes was patented by Chester W. Cook for the first snooze feature in 1914.

The Casio WQV3D-8 Wrist Camera is the first colour-watch combo.

The Zap Lepton is the first fully electric (2001) full-size production scooter, with a top speed of 25 mph and a range of around 20 miles.

Belgian Finance Minister Didier Reynders on September 22, 2001 became the first European to withdraw euro cash from an ATM.

Mademoiselle, a fashion magazine for young women that was first published in 1935 went out of business with the last issue in November 2001.

The Barbie doll first hit store shelves in 1959.

The first museum in U.S. was established in Charleston, S.C. in 1773.

In 1892 the first basketball game was played in Springfield, Massachusetts.

In 1936 "The Green Hornet" was first heard on Detroit radio station WXYZ.

The first U.S. Supreme Court session was held in 1790.

In 1894 New York became the first state to license dogs.

Schick, Inc. introduced the first electric shaver in 1931.

The "Concorde" made its first test flight in 1969.

The first Laundromat was opened in the U.S. in 1934.

The first duck-billed platypus from Australia was first exhibited to the public in 1922.

In 1848 the first women's rights convention was held in Seneca Falls, N.Y.

In 1851 the first issue of the New York Times was issued.

The FU4 Corsair was the first U.S. fighter to fly more than 400 mph with a full military load.

The FH-1 Phantom, a McDonnell aircraft, became the first jet aircraft (1946) to take off from and land on a carrier.

The F/A-18 Hornet was the first naval aircraft in the world so adept at air-to-air and air-to-ground that it was granted dual F/A designation.

The F-8 Crusader by Vought was the first aircraft to set a record of over 1,000 mph and to cross the nation at a velocity greater than the speed of sound.

The AN/SQQ-32 variable depth mine hunting sonar system developed by Raytheon and Thomas-CSF of France was the first sonar to locate and identify live influence-type bottom mines in combat.

In 1895 George B. Seldon received the first U.S. patent for an automobile.

In 1832 the first horse-drawn streetcar began operating in NYC, NY.

The first gorilla born in captivity was in 1956 in Columbus, Ohio.

The Triton was the first nuclear submarine to travel around the world underwater.

Ashley Cadan of Toronto, Canada, a 15 year old amputee, completed a 12-mile swim across Lake Erie late Friday September 7, 2001, making her the youngest woman and first disabled person to accomplish the feat.

In 1957 King Saud became the first Saudi ruler to visit the United States.

When the Taliban was driven from Kabul in November 2001, music was again allowed. The first song played on Radio Afghanistan was Kabul Joan, by Farhad Darya, an Afghan singer in exile since 1990.

In November 2001, four agribusinesses, Archer Daniels Midland, Cargill, Riceland Foods, and ConAgra became the first U.S. companies in four decades to sign trade accords with Cuba.

General Atomics RQ-1 Predator was the first to be deployed in Bosnia in 1995. The Predator was the first unmanned aircraft (UAV) to see combat in Afghanistan in November 2001.

Elvis Presley is the ONLY singer to be inducted into all three singing Halls of Fame—Country, Rock n' Roll and Gospel.

Claudia Haignere became the first French woman in space on October 21, 2001. The 44-year-old blasted off from the Baikonur Cosmodrome in the former Soviet Republic of Kazakstan as a crew engineer—the first non-Russian female to do so.

In 1912 Edwin Howard Armstrong created one of the first effective amplitude modulated (AM) receivers, opening the door to commercial broadcasting.

In 1924 the first mobile radio telephone was demonstrated from a Model T, and New York City police cars were equipped with mobile communications.

Philo T. Farnsworth transmitted the first television image in 1927.

The first communications satellite was launched into orbit in 1963.

The first cellular phones made their debut in Japan in 1979.

The first time in 46 years, 2001's Halloween ghosts and goblins went trick or treating by the light of a full moon. The next chance to see this again will be the year 2020.

In 1974 Richard Nixon became the first U.S. President to visit Saudi Arabia.

President John F. Kennedy commissioned the first Seal's team in 1962.

In 1957 a dog named Laika became the first creature to orbit Earth in the Soviet Sputnik 2 satellite.

Carl Vinson (D. Ga.) served in Congress for 50 years. The first living American to have a Navy ship named in his honour (in 1980), he died in 1981 at 97.

Franklin Delano Roosevelt (FDR) in 1932, the governor of New York attended the Democratic convention in Chicago, thus becoming the first President to go to his party's convention to accept its nomination in person.

James Garfield was the ONLY minister elected U.S. President.

Mikhail Gorbachev, former head of the Soviet Union, was the first recipient of the Ronald Reagan Freedom Award for service to freedom-loving people around the world.

UNIVAC, the world's first commercial computer, was first used June 14, 1951. UNIVAC cost between $1 million and $1.5 million to build weighed eight tons and was powered by vacuum tubes instead of microprocessors.

In 1966 cycling became the first sport to introduce drub testing as a result of Danish cyclist Knut Jensen in 1960.

Makiko Tanaka made her first visit to the U.S. on June 18, 2001. She is Japan's first female foreign minister.

Aton Peters was the first missing child to appear on a milk carton.

Drug Kingpin Juan Raul Gaiza was the first person executed (June 19, 2001) under the 1988 federal Anti-Drug Abuse Act, which imposes a death sentence for murders stemming from drug trafficking.

In 1997 Desmond Richardson became the American Ballet Theatre's first Black principal dancer.

The first passenger rail service (10 mph) in the U.S. started in 1826.

The first Model T Ford came off the line in 1908 for a bargain price of $850. In 1903 Ford Motor Co. ONLY had $223.65 in the bank.

The first tuxedo was worn in 1886 in the U.S.

In 1929 for the first time a baby was born in an airplane.

New York City held its first ticker-tape parade in 1919.

The first to navigate the Colorado River was Major John Wesley Powell.

The Holland Tunnel that linked New York to New Jersey under the Hudson River was the first tunnel in the world designed specifically for motor traffic. On November 12, 1927 for the first and ONLY time pedestrians were officially allowed through the tunnel.

Princess Margaret, sister of Queen Elizabeth II of England died at the age of 71 in February 2002. Her body was cremated making her the first member of the royal family to have their body cremated.

In October of 2001, Daniel Carson Lewis fired a bullet into the trans-Alaska pipeline, causing a large oil spill and forcing its shutdown. The attack was the first time the 4-foot-diameter steel pipeline has ever been pierced by a bullet.

Georgia's highest court struck down the use of the electric chair October 5. 2001. The ruling is believed to be the first time a state's highest court has struck down use of the electric chair as cruel and unusual.

J. M. Smucker was founded in 1897, when the company's namesake and founder sold his first product—apple butter—from the back of a horse drawn wagon.

In 1975 William a. Smith of Bucks County, Pennsylvania was elected the first U.S. president of The International Association of Plastic Arts, the UNESCO art association.

Theodore Roosevelt was probably the ONLY chief executive to pack a revolver in self-defense.

Homestala Mining Co. was incorporated in 1877 and became the first gold offering on the New York Stock Exchange two years later.

Theodore Roosevelt was the first U.S. President to invite an African-American to dinner at the White House and the first American recipient of the Nobel Peace Prize.

LaGuardia was the first mayor of New York City to live in Gracie Mansion.

The first time the U.S. began using nicknames was during WWII as both propaganda and a security tactic.

The first robot plane designed specifically to carry weapons into combat, (Boeing X-45A, White-and-Blue UCAV) completed its initial tests (December 2001) as expected made a maiden flight in early 2002.

Warren G. Harding was the first U.S. President to hire official speechwriter, Judson Welliver, in 1921, titling Literary Executive Secretary to the President.

Elizabeth Blockwell graduated first in her class from Geneva Medical College, N.Y. and became the first woman doctor of modern time in the United States.

Europe's euro first became legal tender at midnight December 31, 2001 on tiny Reunion Island, a French department in the Indian Ocean.

For the first time (2000-2001) in modern history or perhaps ever, the Supreme Court of the United States decided more cases by a 5-4 vote than by a unanimous vote.

A patient on the brink of death received the world's first (July 2001) self-contained artificial heart—a battery-powered device the size of a softball that runs without the need for wires, tubes or hoses sticking out of the chest.

The ONLY river in the world that flows backwards is the one in Chicago.

When a military mission requires secrecy, SEALs often are the first to be called. In recent years, they have been ordered to rescue a downed American pilot in Yugoslavia as well as a deposed Haitian leader.

A law-approved unanimously by the legislature and signed by Gov. John G. Roland of Connecticut (June 2001)—prohibits teachers, counselors, and other school officials from recommending psychiatric drugs for any child. This was a first-in-the-U.S. law.

Arica, Chile in the Atacama Desert receives .03 inches of precipitation per year. Rainfall occurs ONLY two or four times a century.

The federal government sued Wal-Mart Stores Inc., (May 2001), the largest U.S. retailer, for allegedly failing to report serious injuries linked to exercise gliders it sold. This is the first time the government safety agency has pursued a retailer for alleged failure to report product-related injuries.

U.S. District Judge Christina A. Snyder on June 7, 2001 held American Airlines and British West Indies Airlines responsible in the death of Caroline Neischer, 75, who was traveling from Los Angeles to Guyana. It was the first time an airline has been held liable for a death because of mishandled luggage.

Deaths from lung cancer overtook breast cancer for the first time (June 2001) among British women, making it the biggest female cancer killer.

The ONLY cathedral built in France during the 20th century can be found in the city of Evry, near Paris.

Gov. George Pataki of New York signed into law June 28, 2001 the U.S. first statewide legislation banning the use of hand-held cell phones by drivers.

Christopher Columbus first spotted the British Virgin Islands in 1493.

The ONLY foods you should eat with your fingers in France are French fires, asparagus, frog legs and raw shellfish.

Locke, California, the ONLY town in the United States built by and for Chinese Americans, goes back to 1915 when an earlier settlement in nearby Walnut Grove burned down and leaders of the displaced community leased 10 acres from landowner George Locke.

A fist-sized meteorite, one of ONLY 18 rocks on Earth known to have come from Mars (June 2001), was found by Swiss scientists in the Oman desert—a prize discovery that could help determine whether the planet ever sustained life.

Conjoined twins from the Maltese island of Gozo in the Mediterranean were brought to London, England December 2000 for separation. One must die so the other can live. This is the first time a British court had been asked to accelerate the death of one person in order to offer the chance of life to another.

Boeing officials gave the first jet the number 707 simply because it was catchy. From then on, the company has continued with the 7X7 numbering scheme for constituency and name in recognition.

Iowa is the ONLY state (2001) in the U.S. that has succeeded banning surcharges at ATMs.

Zero is the ONLY number that, when added to itself, equals itself.

We are the ONLY species able to change the natural world and able to understand what we've done, so we must be the stewards of the world.

Not ONLY has breastfeeding been shown to be good for children, infants who have been on the breast also having better eyesight than those who have not.

Americans are good at adjusting to reality—pragmatism is the ONLY true native philosophy—and the surging reality is of a technological and economic system without boundaries

Humans, it turns out, have ONLY about twice as many genes as fruit flies or earthworms, and almost the same number as cornstalks.

Protection of civil liberties is often the FIRST casualty of fear.

Bob Marley and the Wailer's first album for Island Records in 1972 was "Catch a Fire".

Sir John A. Macdonald was Canada's first prime minister.

Susan Butcher is the ONLY woman to have won the Alaskan sled-dog race (The Iditarod), four (4) times.

Geraldine Apponyi the first queen of American descent was married to King Zog I of Albania.

In Mary Shelly's novel, Victor is the first name of Dr. Frankenstein.

In 1980, for the first time in over 120 years, Mt. Helen erupted.

By the end of April 1866 former U.S. President Jefferson Davis was the ONLY confederate official still held prisoner.

The first professional game in football was played in Latrobe, Pennsylvania in August of 1895.

The first Chief Justice of the U.S., John Jay, died in Bedford, New York, in 1829.

It took nine years to finish a 1,200-foot passage below the Thames River in London—the first underwater tunnel in the world.

In January 1994 the first combo cell phone—PDA was introduced.

Sloboden Milosevic is the first head of state to face an international tribunal; Milosevic faces a total of 66 counts of genocide and other war crimes in Croatia, Bosnia and Kosovo.

The first discover of a black hole, Cygnus X-1, was made in 1972.

Jose Ferrer was the first Hispanic to win the Academy Award for best actor.

The USS Holland (named after designer John P. Holland) was the U.S. Navy's first submarine.

Minnesota Twin Larry Hisle became baseballs' first designated hitter in a spring training game in 1973.

The first traffic signals, installed between 1910 and 1920, had ONLY red and green lights, mimicking railroad signal lights.

Bud Greenspan directed Denzel Washington in his first TV movie, The Wilma Rudolph Story.

In 1795 Jose Quervo received the first permit from Spain to produce tequila.

Sylvester "Pat" Weaver created the first early morning show, "Today", in 1952, with host Dave Garroway.

Marjorie Knoller of San Francisco was convicted on March 21, 2002 of second-degree murder because her dog killed a neighbor. It was the first murder conviction in a dog-mauling case in California and was believed to be ONLY the third of its kind in recent U.S. history.

Warren Harding, the first rock climber to scale Yosemite's Il Capitan, opened the door to 'big wall" climbing in the U.S. Harding died at age 77 March 2002.

A 1940' passenger plane once owned by Haitian Papa Doc Duvalier and now owned by the Smithsonian Institution is the ONLY Boeing 307 Stratoliner still in existence.

The "interceptor baby armor" was worn by U.S. troops in Afghanistan for the first time in the war against terrorists in 2002.

In 1953 Sir Edmund Hillard scaled Mount Everest wearing a Rolex steel Oyster Perpetual Explorer—making it the first watch to reach the highest point on earth.

The Omega steel Speedmaster Moonwatch, worn by Neil Armstrong in 1969, was the first timepiece to reach the moon.

In 1947 Barbara Wasburn became the first woman to summit Mount McKinley.

The world's first attack submarine H.L. Hunley was a 40-footer fashioned out of an old boiler by Confederate soldiers during the Civil War.

The USS Nautilus SSN 571 (1954) was the world's first nuclear submarine. This 319 foot ship was the first to sail to the North Pole (underneath the icecap).

Colonel Wilson L. "Bud" Peck, USMC, was the first Marine Reserve Colonel to serve in Vietnam.

Michael Jackson's first musical video on TV was "Billy Jean".

In 1994 Rachael Swartz became the first female to win the $100,000 Jeopardy Championship.

The weather channel made its first broadcast May 2, 1982.

Jimmy Carter arrived in Cuba on Sunday May 12, 2002 (Mothers Day) and became the first U.S. President—in or out of office—to visit this Communist country since the 1959 revolution that put Fidel Castro in power.

In 1911 a Wright Brothers plane called the Vin Fizz (after a soft drink sponsor) became the first to fly across the U.S., completing the trip in 84 days with 70 stops.

In the winter of 1903 Mary Anderson scribbled a drawing of what would become the first successful windshield wiper system. Charlotte Bridgewood patented the first automatic windshield wiper in 1917.

Gilmore Schjeldahl built Echo1, the first communication satellite, from a mix of Mylar and adhesive.

In 1975 Francisco Xavier do Amaral was appointed as first president of East Timor.

In 1996 Senator Tim Hutchinson, a GOP member, became the first Republican elected to the Senate from Arkansas since 1879. He divorced his wife of 29 years and married a former aide. Hutchinson voted to convict President Clinton.

Former left-wing (soccer) firebrand Paul Boateng made British history when he took over the #2 job at Treasury (May 2002) as Britain's first Black Cabinet Minister.

Canada was the first nation to pull its soldiers out of Afghanistan's ground war.

Princess Anne of England wore a uniform at her grandmother's funeral. She's the first woman in British history to walk in a royal funeral procession.

The F-22 Raptor, the world's first stealth air-to-air fighter, will enter service with the U.S. Air Force in late 2005.

Alex Perry was named by the Vietnam Memorial Fund as the first recipient of its War Correspondent Award in May 2002 for his duties in the Afghan war.

Indra Devi was renowned gura Sri Krishnamacharya's first women student. She died at age 102 in May 2002.

Ruth Handler is co-founder of Mattel and creator of Barbie, the first mass-marketed American doll with adult curves.

The Boeing Model 314 Clipper was the flying boat that made the first scheduled trans-Atlantic flight in 1939.

In 1919 the Carnegie hired Edwin Hubble, who first confirmed that celestial bodies known as nebulae were actually galaxies outside our own.

Ann Landers the columnist whose real name was Esther Lederer died in June 2002. Her column first appeared in print October 16, 1955, in the Chicago Sun-Times.

Cleveland was the first and ONLY U.S. President to marry in the White House.

Dr. Julie Gerberding is the first female director of the Center for Disease Control and Prevention (CDC)—July 2002.

Steve Fossett, an American investment adventurer millionaire ended his 19,428.6 mile journey on July 2, 2002—becoming the first person to fly a balloon solo around the world. Fossett holds world records in ballooning, sailing and flying airplanes. He has an MBA degree, swam the English Channel in 1985, placed 47th in the Iditarod dog sled race in 1992, and participated in the 24 Hours of Le Mans car race in 1996.

Swiss pilot Bertrand Piccard and Englishman Brian Jones made the first round-the-world balloon voyage in March 1999 through the Northern Hemisphere.

In 1981 John Pazsgai of Morrisville, Pennsylvania became the first person in the United States to go to prison for violating the federal Clean Water Act.

Hassium was first produced by nuclear physicists in 1984. Hassium does not occur naturally.

In the early 1800's, lumps of spruce resin came to be the first commercial chewing gum marketed in the U.S.

The first human uterine transplant was performed in March 2002. The surgery performed in Saudi Arabia, involved the transfer of a uterus from an old donor into a 26-year-old woman whose uterus had been removed because of hemorrhaging.

One of the first things anyone without kids should learn before planning an estate is the difference between a WILL and a TRUST. A Trust, unlike a traditional Will, is not subject to probate expenses should there be any disputes among beneficiaries.

U.S. chickens are known as "Bush legs" in Russia because they were first imported in 1989 under the first President Bush.

The team that scores 100 points first during a basketball game normally wins the game.

Jesse James robbed his first train in July 1873.

Andre-Jacques Garmerin performed the first parachute jump on October 22, 1797.

John William Draper took the first picture of the moon in 1839.

Kemmonds Wilson (born 1913) became fed up with rundown motels he encountered on family road trips, quit his job selling popcorn to cinemas to build the first Holiday Inn.

John W. Backus (born 1924) led a group of IBM engineers who developed the first high-level computer programming language.

Gordon Gould wound up with the patent for LASER—light amplification by stimulated emission of radiation—the intense beams of light were first used for cutting and boring metals and other materials.

Former J.C. Penny management trainee Sam Walton (1918-1992) opened his first Wal-Mart in Rogers, Arkansas—1962.

Gary Kildall created the first operating system for personal computers—nearly a decade before Bill Gates signed his epochal deal with IBM for MS-DOS.

Eunice Grayson was the first actress to play a Bond love interest in two different films:

> Bond girl Silvia Trench in "DR. NO" and "From Russia With Love".

Senator Trent Lott, a Republican from Mississippi resigned as Leader of the Senate in December 2002. Lott resigned after he became the focus of a raging controversy for remarks he made praising Senator Strom Thurmond's 1948 segregationist run for president thus becoming the first Leader of the U.S. Senate to resign.

In 1917 U.S. Rubber introduced Keds, the first mass-marketed rubber-soled sneaker.

In 1923 Roy and Walt Disney made movie goers first experienced the magic with Snow White and the Seven Dwarfs from the multiplane camera.

Mutual fund was founded in 1924 by L.Sherman Adams, Charles H. Learoyd and Ashton L. Carr; Massachusetts Investors Trust became the world's first open-ended investment fund with ONLY $50,000 in capital.

Clark University physicist Robert Hutchings Goddard (1882-1945) launched the first rocket in 1926 from a field near Auburn, Massachusetts.

Fred Thompson, republican from Tennessee, who plays the district attorney on Law and Order, the first sitting U.S. Senator to have a regular TV gig.

Philo Taylor Farnsworth (1906-1971) transmitted the first all-electronic image, a horizontal line in 1927.

In a 1941 test flight the world's first jet reached 370 miles per hour, for faster than propped planes.

Wallace Hume Carothers (1896-1937) earned a professorship at Harvard, then a research job at DuPont. There he created the first synthetic nylon fiber.

Budapest-born physician Bernard Fantus (1874-1940) created the first blood bank at Cook County Hospital in Chicago.

Floyd Carlson (1906-1968), a lawyer, grew tired of making copies of patent applications and law textbooks. In 1946 he struck with Haloid Co., which introduced the first commercial copying machine.

Raytheon engineer Percy L. Spencer (1894-1970) brought kitchens into the space age. In 1947 "Radarange" was the world's first microwave oven.

While working at Harvard Computation Laboratory, Shanghai-born physicist AnWang (1920-1990) created the "pulse transfer controlling device", the first method of storing information on a computer without large magnetic drums.

Ivan the Terrible was crowned as first Russian Czar in January 1547.

Warren G. Harding had the first radio installed in the White House on February 8, 1922.

Senator Robert Kennedy was the first to reach the summit of Mt. Kennedy in Yukon Territory in March 1965.

Morris S. Frank was the first person to be presented with a seeing eye dog in April 1928.

Henry Ford took his first car, quadricycle, for a test drive in June 1896.

John Archer became the first person to receive the Bachelor of Medicine degree in the U.S. in 1761.

Dr. Emily Stowe became the first woman in 1880 to practice medicine in Canada.

Democrat Frank Lautenberg of New Jersey is the first U.S. Senator to resign from office, entered the 2002 election late and defeated Douglas Forrester.

Lane Vestergaard Hau, professor of Applied Physics, Harvard University, was the first to bring light, (which moves at a constant breakneck pace of 186,282 miles per second in a vacuum) to a screeching halt.

During her research career Maxine Singer, a molecular biologist, has investigated the organization of the human genome and helped draft the first safety guidelines for genetic engineering.

Jocelyn Bell Burnell, with the aid of a radio telescope she built herself, became the first astronomer to detect pulsars—rapidly spinning, extremely dense neutron stars.

The spaceship Endeavour took astronaut John Harrington, the first American Indian into space, and four others November 2002.

Barr Nelson first played James Bond in a 1954 teleplay of "Casino Royale".

The late William Holden was the first Hollywood star to break the million-dollar barrier earning $1 million in 1957 for "The Bridge on the River Kwai."

Prime Minister P.J. Patterson prime minister of Jamaica and leader of the Peoples National Party (PNP) became the first leader elected to three straight terms after winning the election on October 16, 2002.

First in nuclear warfare:

In 1945 U.S. drops the first atomic bombs on Hiroshima and Nagasaki, killing more than 120,000.

> In 1949 the USSR tests its first nuclear weapon.
> In 1952 The UK tests its first nuclear weapon.
> In 1960 France tests its first nuclear weapon.
> In 1964 China tests its first nuclear weapon.
> In 1974 India tests its first nuclear weapon.
> In 1998 Pakistan tests its first nuclear weapon.

John D. Rockefeller founder of Standard Oil, built the U.S. first multi-national corporation and is also the first person in America to become a billionaire.

William Bodde Jr., was the Asia-Pacific Economic Cooperation's (APEC) first executive director.

Desmond Llewelyn died in a car crash in 1999. "Die Another Day" is the first Bond movie since "Live and Let Die" that never feature him.

In 1967 Katherine Switzer became the first woman to officially enter The Boston Marathon, and she did so by registering as "K. Switzer" to mask her gender.

In 296 B.C. Princess Kyniska of Sparta became the first female champion, in chariot racing, much to the chagrin of her male competitors.

E. Burke Wilford's twin outrigger pylons reflected some of the aerodynamic thinking seen a few years after 1934 in the German FA-61, considered the first successful helicopter.

Rep. Michael Myers, D. Pa., (1980) and Ohio Rep. James Traficant (2002) are the ONLY tow member of The U.S. House of Representatives to be expelled from The House since the Civil War. Traficant was sentenced to (8) years in jail.

Oxana Fedorova, a 24-year-old student became the first (2002) Miss Universe to be ousted after winning the contest.

In 1806 Webster published its first dictionary.

Venezuela is the ONLY country on the South American continent that's an OPEC member.

Linda Hunt is the ONLY performer to win an acting Oscar for a role in a Gibson film—"The Year of Living Dangerously".

Harrison Ford and Liam Neeson face a nuclear melt-down aboard a Soviet submarine in "K-19: The Widowmaker", National Geographic's first feature film.

Elvis Presley is maybe the ONLY person Americans celebrate his death on his death date.

Oprah Winfrey was the first person to receive the Bob Hope Humanitarian Award that was given at the 2002 5th annual Emmys.

President Vladimir Putin of Russia was the first foreign leader to talk by telephone to U.S. President George W. Bush after the September 11, 2001 attacks.

In 1945 at age 10, Elvis Presley made his first appearance in a talent show at the Mississippi-Alabama Fair and Dairy Show, singing "Old Shep". He won second place and $5.

David Eisenhower is the ONLY person whose grandfather was a U.S. President and he was married to Julie Nixon whose father was Richard Nixon, another U.S. President and also Vice President to Eisenhower.

New York City is the ONLY city in the world that taxes rent as of year 2002.

Lake Ontario is the ONLY one of the great lakes that does not border Michigan State.

The first commercially developed car radio was by Motorola.

In 1959 Elizabeth Taylor became the first actress to earn $1 million for a film—Cleopatra.

ONLY two actress have won the Oscar back-to-back. Luise Rainer in 1936 and 1937 and Katherine Hepburn in 1967 and 1968. Hepburn is also the ONLY performer with four Oscars.

In 1562, Sir John Hawkins led the first slave ships from West Africa to America via Europe.

Hurricane Bob in 1979 was the first Atlantic hurricane with a male name.

Kathleen McGrath was the first woman ever to command a U.S. Navy Warship. She died of cancer in October 2002.

Patsy Mink, a Hawaii liberal Democrat was the first Asian-American woman elected to the U.S. Congress. She died In October 2002.

Frederick Law Olmsted, who died in 1903, became America's first and greatest landscape architect.

James Rodger Fleming is a professor of science, technology, and society at Colby College in Waterville, Maine and founder and first president of the International Commission on the History of Meteorology.

Ilan Ramon, a colonel in Israel's air force and a combat pilot became the first Israeli astronaut on January 16, 2003. Colonel Ramon on board the shuttle Columbia never made it back to Earth. February 1, 2003, the shuttle disintegrated 200,000' up on its way to land in Florida after 16 days in space. The Columbia was first launched in 1981.

Judge William Webster is the ONLY CIA Chief to have also served as the Director of the FBI.

Richard Bissell was the manager of the stunning operation to build the U-2, the first high-altitude spy plane.

Former Pennsylvania Governor Tom Ridge was sworn in on Friday January 24, 2003 as the first head of the new Homeland Security Department—a new Cabinet post.

Roald Amundsen in 1906 became the first explorer to survive a crossing of the Northwest Passage, a deadly maze of sea ice, narrow straits and misshapen islands.

Japanese Emperor Akihito was operated on in January 2003 to remove his prostrate gland. Akihito was the first Japanese

Emperor to undergo surgery at a public hospital rather than in his palace.

Laura and Jim Richardson (both from Ft. Campbell, Ky.) and both helicopter pilots, saw war duty in Iraq; they made Army history as the first husband-and-wife team to command battalions in the same brigade task force.

Osaka's Fusae Ota is Japan's first female governor elected in 2000, the Japanese Sumo Association has banned her from their ring. Tradition states that under no circumstances are women to enter the Dohyo, Sumo's Ring.

Theodore Roosevelt signed an executive order in February 1903 creating Pelican Island Reservation, the first federal bird preserve and the first piece of the vast patchwork of sanctuaries know as The National Wildlife Refuge System.

Elgen Long in 1971 is the ONLY person to have traveled solo from the South Pole to the North Pole, a 32,000-mile trip.

Christopher Columbus was the first European to try his hand at transplanting a religion to the Islands of the Bahamas.

PFC Jessica Lynch, a member of the 507th Maintenance Company, was held captive as a Prisoner of War (POW) in Iraq in March 2003. She was freed by U.S. special operations soldiers on April 1, 2003 thus becoming the first POW freed from captivity since WWII.

U.S. Army PFC Lori Piestewa, an American Indian was the first female combat death in the Iraqi War in April 2003.

Michael Kelly, editor-at-large for the Atlantic Monthly, was killed while covering the war in Iraq (April 2003), was the first American journalist to die in the conflict.

Abu Hamza al-Masri, a Muslim cleric, had his British citizenship revoked (April 2003) because he applauded the September 11, 2002 attacks on the United States. Masri is the first person targeted under new measures aimed at deporting immigrants whose words or actions are deemed to "seriously prejudice" British interests.

In 1980 Italian Reinhold Messner scores an unprecedented feat by becoming the first person to climb Mt. Everest without supplemental oxygen or a radio.

Acadia National Park located primarily on Mount Desert Island was the first national park established east of the Mississippi.

Dodge Morgan took 150 days to sail around the world solo in 1986 and became the first American to do so.

Eileen Collins grew up in public housing in Elmira, N.Y. She was NASA's first female shuttle pilot (in 1995) and commander (in 1999).

The Roosevelt Hotel in Los Angeles, California was built in 1927; it had the first Academy Awards Ceremony in 1929.

Rebecca Martinez of Santo Domingo, Dominican Republic was born on December 10, 2003 with the undeveloped head of her twin, an extremely rare condition known as craniopagus parasiticus. Rebecca was ONLY the eighth documented case in the world of craniopagus parasiticus.

South Korean scientists described on February 12, 2004 how they cloned several human embryos and extracted valuable stem cells from one. They are the first researchers to prove they cloned a human being.

Edouard Manet was the first painter to paint scenes of modern life rather than paint the stories of classical mythology.

The Robert Hall of Fame created in 2003 at Carnegie Mellon University, inducted its first members in November 2003.

The 650-horsepower Toyota Tundras thundering around Daytona International Speedway January 2004 at 190 mph; become the first foreign automaker to crash the emphatically American party of NASCAR.

The Korean War—the first major armed clash between Free World and Communist forces—turned the so-called "Cold War" hot, with a divided country's fight over its borders, eventually engaging world powers.

General George Washington created The Badge of Military Merit, represented by the figure of a heart cut from purple cloth—America' first military decoration.

The USS Reuben James was the first U.S. Navy ship sunk during hostile action in World War II.

The first Los Angeles—class submarine was commissioned in 1976 and the latest in 1996.

First commissioned in 1981, the Ohio-class submarines are nuclear-powered and virtually undetectable.

World War I (WWI) is regarded as the first "total war" because the combatants devoted all their resources—military, industrial and human—on a scale never before thought possible.

The Medical College of Pennsylvania (MCP) was closed in 2004 after 153 years. This hospital was the United States first medical school for women and has been serving the Philadelphia community since the Civil War.

Idaho Gem, born May 4, 2003 was the first successful cloning of an equine. He was followed by siblings Utah Pioneer on June 9th and Idaho Star on July 27th.

R. Gorden Wasson (1898-1986) became the first White man known experiment with mushroom (psychedelic mushrooms). He and a friend traveled to a remote Mexican village in 1955 and took up with Shaman Maria Sabina.

Randy Cunningham (now a U.S. Congressman in 2000) was the first ace of the Viet Nam War.

The Earth Liberation Front (ELF), a militant underground environmental group, first surfaced in the United States in 1996 by setting fire to a U.S. Forest Service truck in Oregon.

Del Martin founded the U.S. first lesbian organization in 1955.

Borge Ousland was the first to ski alone and unsupported from Siberia to the North Pole.

George Bush, is the U.S.A.'s first MBA President.

Each year, the human-rights group Freedom House ranks every country according to its level of political rights and civil liberties. North Korea (head of state Kim Jong II since 1994) is the ONLY nation to earn the worst possible score for 31 years.

Robert Mugabe was elected independent Zimbabwe's first prime minister in 1980, with widespread domestic and international support. In 2004 he was rated #4 on the Worst Dictator list.

Joseph Massimo is the ONLY New York Mafia Boss in 2004 who isn't doing hard time or awaiting sentencing for a conviction. That makes him the Last Don. The first Mob Lord executed by the state was Murder Inc's Louis (Lepke) Buchalter, electrocuted in 1944.

Switzerland, Germany and Belgium trade off for first place from year to year in per capita chocolate consumption.

Ireland is the first country in Europe to prohibit smoking in bars. Tobacco kills half a million EU every year.

Alicia Keys was the first pop star to perform at the elite 18th-century Royal Theatre in Copenhagen, Denmark on June 16, 2004.

Mikhail Gorbachev dissolved the USSR in 1991. Russia's next leader, Boris Yeltsin, was elected as the country's first president.

Harry Belafonte, activist, actor, and performer first gained international acclaim when he released the album Calypso in 1956, which stayed at No. 1 for 31 weeks. From it came his biggest hit "Day-O (The Banana Boat Song)".

When chess was first played, around the 6th century in India the bishop was an elephant, the rook a chariot. The king was a shah, and next to him stood not a queen but a vizier, or chief counselor, able to move ONLY one square at a time.

On April 26, 1954, scientists delivered what was called "the shot felt around the world". In the cafeteria of Franklin Sherman Elementary School in McLean, VA., a young physician gave the first inoculation of a vaccine developed by Dr. Jonas Salk.

Hollywood got two stars for the price of one (April 2004) as 17-year old twins Mary-Kate and Ashley Olsen shared a new marker on the Walk of Fame. These were the first twins to be so honoured.

Norris McWhirter died in April 2004 from a heart attack. In 1954 he compiled the first Guinness World Records with his twin brother, Ross.

National Public Radio's Bob Edwards signed off as host of Morning Edition in May 2004. The first person he spoke with when Morning Edition was launched in 1979 was Charles Osgood of CBS News.

The British satirical magazine Punch was first published in 1841.

Claude (Fiddler) Williams died in May 2004. He was Count Basie's first recorded guitarist and a master of jazz violin.

Campbell's has introduced limited-edition cans in four combination soups, selling for $2.99 in May 2004, a four-pack exclusively at Giant Eagle supermarkets. This is the first time Campbell's has deviated from its red-and-white label since it was introduced in 1898.

The Philips Keyring Camcorder is the first USB gadget sold in the U.S. with a video camera, still camera and MP3 player all inside a single unit about the size of a breakfast sausage.

DDT was the first man-made insecticide, it was first marketed in 1944.

William Horlick produced the first malted milk in 1882.

New York City (NYC) was the first Capital of the United States.

Nuthatches are the ONLY American birds that can walk headfirst down a tree.

Galileo first demonstrated that air has weight.

The Apaches were the first Indians to own horses.

Michigan was the first state to abolish the death penalty—in 1847.

John Adams was the first president to live in the White House.

Marvin Runyon died in May 2004. He was 79. Runyon began his career in 1943 at a Ford plant in Dallas, Texas, where he climbed to the post of vice-president before leaving in 1980 to become Japanese automaker Nisson's first employee in the U.S.

TV Guide first debuted on April 3, 1952. It cost 15 cents and its first cover featured Lucy and Desi's baby, Desi Arnaz Jr.

Polish monks first made crude vodka more than five centuries ago.

McCarron International in Las Vegas in 2004 became the first airport to attach radio-frequency identification (RFID) to baggage.

Michigan was the first state to develop roadside parks and picnic tables.

In 1948 John Curtis and his brother manufactured the first chewing gum in the U.S. in Bangor, Maine.

The '39 Oldsmobile was first to feature an automatic transmission.

Freud first lectured in the U.S. in 1909.

Danish Crown Prince Frederik married Australian commoner Mary Donaldson on Friday May 14, 2004. Mary became the first Australian woman to stand in line to become queen.

John Quincy Adams and Dwight D. Eisenhower were the ONLY two U.S. Presidents that were bald.

On July 5, 1954 Elvis Presley recorded his first single, "That's All Right" in Memphis.

Crown Prince Felipe of Spain married former TV anchorwoman Letizia Ortiz on Saturday May 22, 2004. Ortiz became the first commoner ever to be in line to be queen. It was Spain's first royal wedding since 1906.

Venus crosses directly in front of the sun ONLY twice a century—on June 8, 2004 this event happened for the first time since 1882.

Paul MacCreary, regarded as the world's greatest living engineer in 2004, built the world's first solar-powered airplanes (Gossamer Penguin and Solar Challenger) and a solar-powered flier (Helios) for the National Aeronautics and Space Administration (NASA).

Ronald Reagan died in June 2004. He was one of 28 people accorded the honor of lying state in the Capitol Rotunda. It is a privilege determined by the U.S. Congress and was first offered to Henry Clay in 1852.

JetBlue pilot crews store their manuals on laptop computers allowing information to be updated instantly, creating the industry's first "paperless cockpit"—June 2004.

Expo 2005 Aichi Japan which ran from March 25 to September 25, 2005 was the first World Exposition of the 21st century. Inside the Japanese Government pavilion, the world's first completely spherical movie screen will display the current state of the Earth and demonstrate changes to global environment.

Energizer Battery markets the first disposable Li-ion AA in 1992.

Gillette makes the first battery-powered disposable razor—the vibrating handle, the company says, emits pulses to prop up stubble—in May 2004.

On May 25, 2001, Erik Weihenmayer became the first blind man in history to reach the summit of Mt. Everest. On September 5, 2002, when he stood on top of Mt Kosciusko in Australia, Erik completed his seven-year quest to climb the Seven Summits—the highest peaks on each of the seven land continents. He joined a select group of ONLY 100 mountaineers who have accomplished that feat.

James Houck and Bill Wilson were the founders of Alcoholics Anonymous (AA) in 1939. Houck is the ONLY living person (he was 90 in 2004) to have attended Oxford Group meetings with Wilson, who died in 1971.

ESPN came on the air on September 7, 1979. Before ESPN viewers were sated by Saturday afternoon ONLY college football, "Wide World of Sports" and three-minute sports report on local news. And so the most enduring of famous first words may prove to be those spoken on September 7, 1979. "If you're a fan", said Sports Center anchor Lee Leonard, in the first utterance ever on ESPN, "What you'll see in the next minutes, hours and days to follow may convince you you've gone to sports heaven".

The Book of Mormon was first published in 1830.

Julia Child was America's first TV Chef. She died on Friday August 13, 2004 three days short of her 92nd birthday.

In the ONLY election since he assumed power in 1994, North Korean dictator Kim Jong II got 100 percent of the vote.

Bill Maher was the man who cracked the first AIDS joke on a network (to Carson: "I just want to meet an old-fashioned girl with gonorrhea") later single-handedly reintroduced political comedy to mainstream.

Gov. James E. McGreevy of New Jersey announced his resignation Thursday August 12, 2004 saying he is a gay American and that he shamefully engaged in adult consensual affairs with another man., McGreevy thus became the first Governor of a state to publicly admit that he is a homosexual.

The National Jewelry, a new nonprofit organization opened its inaugural show on august 20, 2004 at the American Folk Art Museum in New York City. The exhibition is the first museum retrospective of American jewelry—each of its 150 pieces was manufactured in the U.S.

The First Arab, Islamic Congress in Europe was held in Berlin, Germany on October 1-3, 2004.

Sears, Roebuck and Co. adopted a new logo, ONLY the fourth in its 118-year history, the logo is brighter blue than its predecessor.

The Toronto International Film Festival (TIFF) has become the unofficial opening for Oscar season. Last year (2003) Lost in Translation, The Cooler and 21 Grams used TIFF as their first shot at an Academy close-up.

Toronto surgeon Robert Jackson was the first North American to use arthroscopic surgery, in the early 1970's, called arthroscopy the greatest orthopedic development of this half of the century. Today 95% of arthroscopic patients go home hours after leaving the operating room and can begin their rehab within days.

Astroturf was invented in 1964. First dubbed ChemGrass when it was laid over the concrete floor of Houston's Astrodome in 1966 this cutting-edge carpet was later given the more Jetsonian handle, AstroTurf.

Richard Nixon and J.F. Kennedy had their first TV debuts in September 1960.

The Vatican in its first (September 2004) speech ever to the U.N. General Assembly, called for a total ban on human cloning and criticized the war in Iraq and unilateral responses to terrorism.

The very first session of Congress on September 7, 1974 began with a three-hour prayer and that even today, every session of Congress begins with a prayer led by a preacher whose salary has been paid by the taxpayers since 1777.

One signer of the U.S. Declaration of Independence, Francis Hopkinson, authored America's first purely American hymn book.

Aaron Burr, third vice president of the United States, was the first vice president not to become president.

Michael Melvill, the test pilot who flew Space Ship One into space and back on June 21, 2004, was awarded the U.F. first commercial astronaut wings by the Federal Aviation Administration (FAA).

Prince Charles, first born son of Queen Elizabeth II, has been the future King of England since his birth 56 years ago (its now year 2004). Two marriage, two sons and 11 Prime Ministers later, he's still waiting.

Jean Rath Hay died in October 2004 at age 87. She was the world's first global disk jockey, who woke millions of American troops during WWII with her plucky Reveille with Beverly program.

Sherry Lansing, chairperson of Paramount Pictures group in 2004 smashed the industry's glass ceiling in 1980 when she became the first woman to head production at a major studio.

Varenincline produced by Pfizer is the first non-nicotine agent developed to help smokers quit. The pills activate the nicotine receptor fooling the smoker into thinking his craving has been satisfied.

Copyright laws first emerged in response to Gutenberg's printing press. The city of Venice in 1476 limited publication of certain books ONLY to those 'privileges'.

The first Coca-Cola advertising clocks reportedly were made around 1891 by Edward Baird, who began manufacturing clock cases in Montreal, Canada, in 1888 to hold clock works that had been made by other companies.

George Bush, is the first U.S. President since Herbert Hoover to preside over an absolute decline in employment in his first four years on the job.

The Netherlands was the first country to legalize euthanasia for terminally ill people.

Christopher Reeve died on Sunday October 10, 2004 from cardiac arrest after years of suffering from a spinal cord injury from a horse accident. Reeve was the choice for the title role in the first "Superman" movie in 1978. About the age of 10 he made his first appearance—in Gilbert and Sullivan's "The Yeoman of Guard" at McCarter Theatre in Princeton, New Jersey.

Ontario, Canada on Friday October 15, 2004 became the first province in Canada to announce plans to ban the pit bull breed.

Harmonix created the first sports game that watches body movement to control your on-screen character.

Sony QUALIA KSX-46x005 is the world's most expensive LCD TV is the first to shine LED light through each pixel rather than using fluorescent strips to illuminate the 46 inch screen.

Divers from police and fire departments got together at the Panama City campus of Florida State University to take part in the first (October 2004) comprehensive training program for underwater crime-scene investigations.

Chicago will get $1.5 billion in a deal to let a private consortium operate the Chicago Skyway toll road. The deal marks the first time a U.S. toll road has been privatized.

General Motors (GM) has an estimated $4.6 billion in revenue in China in 2004. It's the first foreign carmaker with a license to provide financing.

Hornets Nest, a novel written by Jimmy Carter is the ONLY novel ever written by a U.S. President.

The DX 7590 takes technology a step further as the first 5MP camera that combines a Schneider-Kreuznach Variogen 10X optical zoom lens and the innovative Kodak color sciences image-processing chip with the ease of use that's became the hallmark of the Kodak Easy Share system.

Leo Hendrik who came to America at 26, was the creator (in 1907) and manufacturer of Bakelite, the first man made plastic and the first true synthetic.

Edwin Howard Armstrong first demonstrated his invention of frequency modulation—FM—in 1935. Armstrong started the first FM station on July 18, 1939.

The Mini Cooper, which first appeared in the United States in 2002, is owned and designed by Germany's BMW but is built in Britain, where the original Mini was conceived back in the 1960's.

The $2.2 billion, nuclear-powered USS Virginia launched in October 2004 differs from other submarines because it can not ONLY roam the deep ocean but can also get close to shore in shallow waters. The 377 foot-long sub is the first to be built without a periscope, using high-resolution digital cameras instead. The sub is the first of 10 Virginia-class submarines scheduled to be built through a partnership between Northrop Grumman Newport News and General Dynamics Electric Boat.

New Zealand, the island nation was the first to give women the right to vote, in 1893. In 2003 Oman allowed all citizens to vote for the first time for a consultative council. Women were granted the right to vote in the U.S. for the first time in 1920, though suffrage was extended to Black males in 1870.

George Washington was the ONLY U.S. President who did not belong to a political party.

Siam, present-day Thailand is the ONLY Southeast Asian country not colonized by a Western power during the 19th century.

Lonnie Dupre undertook the first summer crossing of the Artic Ocean.

In the 20th century ONLY one candidate was elected without winning his home state. Woodrow Wilson lost New Jersey in 1916.

Founded by Osama bin Laden in the 1980 al Qaeda first supported the Mujahidin fighting Soviets in Afghanistan. Today the group wages war on the world, through a global Islamist insurgency.

The cost of a New York City taxi medallion in 1937 was $10.00, the year the licenses were first introduced. In October 2004 a cab driver Mohammed Shad had a winning bid of $360,000 for a taxi medallion, the highest ever paid for an individual license in New York City.

Atlantic City opened its first casino in 1978—Resorts. Donald Trump bought his first casino in 1984.

Lt. Col. Andrew Lourake is the first amputee to fly a U.S. Air Force aircraft.

Julia Morgan graduated in civil engineering from Berkeley in 1894. She applied to and was rejected by the Ecole des Beaux-Arts in Paris. She persisted and finally was accepted, and in 1902 became the first woman to earn its prestigious certificate. Morgan (1892-1957) went on to become one of the United States first female architects, known most famously for Hearst Castle in California.

Shell spent an estimated $2 million in November 2004 for the first hydrogen pump at a public U.S. gas station in Washington.

Thomson and In Focus co-developed the first sub-7-inch rear projection TVs (which are typically less expensive than plasmas or LCDs), shrinking the cabinet depth by utilizing a lens that greatly shortens the focal length and a screen that better focuses light to yield a bright, clear picture with no distortion.

The Braddock Dam in the Monongahela River near Pittsburgh, Pa. is the first dam ever built on dry land using prefab concrete and then snapped into place like some gargantuan Lego project.

The Graceful DA42 Twin Star four-passenger plane is the first light airplane (and the first airplane since the 1930's) designed for diesel power.

Avastin is the first tumor-starving drug approved for cancer treatment. It is first in a new class of drugs known as angiogenesis inhibitors, takes a more strategic approach. Avastin shrinks tumors by blocking protein that stimulates blood vessel growth.

Rimonabant is a drug for losing weight, stop smoking and control cholesterol. It's the first drug to block a chemical receptor called cannabinoid-1, the culprit behind marijuana-induced munchies and other cravings that drive us to overindulge.

Wayne Newton singer, actor, is the first person inducted into Las Vegas Walk of Stars.

George Silk was the first to photograph the city of Nagasaki after the Japanese city was hit by an atom bomb in WWII.

John Mitchell was the first U.S. Attorney General to be convicted of a felony.

Woodrow Wilson, 28th President of the U.S. is the ONLY president buried in Washington, D.C.

Mel Martinez, 58 years old in 2004 and a victory in Florida became the first Cuban-American to be elected to the U.S. Senate.

Marcus Loew born to poor Jewish immigrants on Manhattan's Lower East Side co-founded the company that opened the first theaters in Cincinnati and New York on November 14, 1904.

Takahiro Omori won the CITGO Bassmaster Classic in August 2003 and became the first non American to win the coveted Bassmaster Classic title.

Four-star generals number ONLY 35 in the year 2004 in the combined Army, Marine Corps, Air Force and Navy (in which four-star admirals are the equivalent).

Muslim Eid al-Fitr, the festival to break Ramadan fasting period—it comes on the first day of Shawwai and begins a three-day period of relaxation and celebration.

The Charite' Artificial Disc is expected to receive FDA approval for degenerative disc disease by the end of 2004, making it the ONLY artificial spinal disc available in the U.S.

Kmart Holding Corp. traces its roots back to 1899 when Sebastion S. Kresge opened his first share in Detroit. The company opened its first Kmart store in a suburb of Detroit in 1962. Founder Sebastian S. Kresge died in 1966 at the age of 99. Kmart is now merged with Sears.

The first Sears retail store opened in 1925 in the company's catalog plant on Chicago's West Side.

Gillette's Sensor 3 is the ONLY disposable razor in 2004 with three spring-mounted sensor blades to adjust to every curve of your face.

First predicted by Einstein's general theory of relativity, gravity waves are ripples in the fabric of space-time.

Ontario court approved Canada's first same sex divorce (September 2004) after a judge ruled that the definition of spouse in the country's Divorce Act was unconstitutional.

New Hampshire was the ONLY state in 2004 without a seat belt law for adults.

In 2004, more than four decades after Alan Shephards flight ONLY two Americans have made the jump into space from U.S. soil—both launched not by NASA but by Burt Rutan's tiny company known for building-your-own-airplane.

French President Jacques Chirac's two-visit, which wrapped up November 25, 2004, marked the first to visit Libya by a French Head of State in more than half a century.

In 1911, Sun Yat-sen was elected the Republic of China's first president.

In 1936, the United Auto Workers Union staged its first "sit-down" strike at the Fisher Body Plant No.1 in Flint, Michigan.

In 1956 Elvis Presley began his first recording session for RCA Records. "Heartbreak Hotel" was among the songs he recorded.

Intrinsa is the ONLY sex drug to treat women—and the first drug ever to remedy low sex drive.

The last two C-141 Starlifters in active duty use were retired September 16, 2004. They belonged to the 30th Mobility Wing at McGuire AFB, N.J. Following a first flight on December 1963 the C-141 served as an operational Air Force strategic air lifter for nearly 40 years. The C-141 was the first jet aircraft designed solely as a troop and cargo carrier.

The Ford Presidential Library in Ann Arbor, Michigan is the ONLY presidential library not attached to a museum.

The $100,000 bill, the highest denomination, was printed in 1934 and used ONLY by Federal Reserve banks to transfer money to each other.

Adam is the first man to learn a valuable lesson: women cause problems.

J.C. Hall, future founder of Hallmark sells his first (1910) greeting cards in Kansas City, Missouri.

Biomass is the ONLY renewable alternative to gasoline.

Hydrogen's ONLY by-products are heat and water.

In Nebraska, where electrocution is the ONLY method of execution, they use a 15-second blast of 2,400 volts of electricity.

San Quentin was California's first prison. San Quentin prison was the first in the U.S. to have its own hospital.

The THRUST SSC is the world's fastest car. Racing down a mile of desert in 4.7 seconds in 1977, the THRUST became the first land vehicle to break the sound barrier.

The FETISH is a production electric car and it's the world's first commercially available electric-powered sports coupe.

Warren Harding became the first U.S. President to file income tax return in March 1923.

On March 16, 1995 Norman Thagard became the first American to visit the Russian space station Mir.

George Clinton became the first U.S. Vice President to die in office—April 20, 1812.

Yellowstone National Park was the world's first National Park.

Dwight Eisenhower became the first U.S. President in 1952 to fly in a helicopter. ONLY the president's helicopter is allowed to fly to or from the White House.

Theodore Roosevelt became the first U.S. President to ride in an automobile—August 1902.

Tate and Lyle PLC, the maker of Splenda's key ingredient sucralose, will begin taking new U.S. customers. The company is the world's ONLY manufacturer of sucralose.

The Salvation Army put out their first red kettle during the Christmas season in 1893 in Chicago.

Pioneer 10, launched in 1983 was the first human-created object to leave the solar system.

Skylab was United States first space station; it was launched in 1973 and plunged into the Indian Ocean in 1979.

New Yorkers took their first subway ride in 1904.

Delphi's MyFi for xm service is the first portable satellite radio.

Tungsten shines ONLY when heated to 4,500 degrees Fahrenheit, on energy-sucking process that converts just 5 percent of electricity to visible light.

Japanese scientists announced in August 2004 that a male salmon had spawned trout hatchlings the first report of one species producing offspring of another.

Elleen Miller is the ONLY American woman to have summitted Mt. Everest by two routes.

On October 4, 1959 Russia's Luna 3 was launched toward the moon where it later became the first vehicle to send back images of the moon's far side.

Philip Cortelyou Johnson was the first winner (1979) of the Pritzer Prize, an honor that aspires to be architectures Nobel.

George Washington was the recipient of the first Congressional Gold Medal.

Nicorette gum became the first smoking cessation product to enter NASCAR when GlaxoSmithKline Consumer Healthcare signed a sponsorship deal in January 2005 with Chip Ganassi Racing.

On the morning of January 31,1945 in the French Alsatian village of St. Marie aux Mines, a U.S. Army private in Pennsylvania 28th Infantry Division was marched into a snow courtyard, strapped to a post and shrouded wit a black hood. For fleeing combat a troubled 24-year-old named Eddie Slovik became the ONLY serviceman since the Civil War executed as a deserter.

Violeta Chamorro was the first woman to be directly elected president in Latin America. She defeated Daniel Ortega, the Sandinista president of Nicaragua in 1990. Ortega was reelected in 2006.

In 1990 Bulgaria, Czechoslovakia, Eastern Germany, Hungary and Romania all held their first post-Soviet-domination democratic elections.

Golda Meir and Benjamin Netanyahu are the ONLY two people moved from the United States to Israel and were elected prime minister.

The Zuni American Indians are the ONLY set of people allowed to have the American bald eagle feathers in their possession.

President George W. Bush was named Person of the Year in 2003 and 2004. This is not the first time a President has earned this title twice. Harry Truman, Dwight Eisenhower (first as a general), Lynden Johnson, Richard Nixon, Ronald Reagan and Bill Clinton all share that distinction.

The Kiwi of New Zealand is the ONLY bird in the world that has nostrils at the end of its beak.

Max Factor created the first false eyelash make-up.

Helga Stoeckart came to Caribbean prominence in 1992, had created history by being the first person to file a palimony suit in Jamaica.

Zirconium is second in hardness to diamond.

Ricardo Palmera, wearing handcuffs and a bulletproof vest (December 2004), became the first leader of the Revolutionary Armed Forces of Columbia, or FARC, to be sent for trial in U.S. Federal Court.

Bobby Jindal R-Louisiana, became ONLY the second person (November 2004) of Indian descent elected to the U.S. Congress (the first Rep. Dalip Singh Saund D-Calif., held office from 1957-1963).

Rhode Island became the first state in the U.S. (December 2004) to approve regulations that allow its residents to import cheaper prescription drugs from Canada.

Astronaut Michael Foale became the first Briton to walk in space in 1995 and completed a six-month stint on the international space station in April 2004.

Pennsylvania Turnpike managers began collecting tolls early Thanksgiving Day 2004 as the first strike in the turnpikes 64-year-history entered its second day.

NASA's "scrambler jet" attained a speed of 6,500 mph, the first aircraft to go Mach 9.6, or 2 miles per second.

Sheikha Lubna al Qasimi ditched her job as CEO of Middle Eastern Tech firm to be the first woman to hold a Cabinet position (Minister of Finance) in 2004 since the United Emirates (UAF) was formed in 1971.

Mayor of Pitcairn Island, Brenda Christian, the sole police officer on this 20-sq.-mile island (pop. 47) became its first woman mayor after nearly half of Pitcairn's adult males were convicted of rape in October 2004.

John F. Kennedy's personal doctor, Janet Graham Travell, the first woman to serve as a White House physician.

In 1998 Jim Sanderson was the first to radio-track the Chilean guigna, the smallest cat in the Western hemisphere.

Berry-flavored 7UP PLUS from Cadbury Schweppes is the first 'fortified" (with added calcium and vitamin C) junk food.

Chicago is the first U.S. city to install roof gardens on its municipal buildings, improving air quality.

Connecticut is fighting off an invasion—of plants. It is one of the first states to establish an Invasive Plants Council and enact a ban on invasive plants.

The USS Jimmy Carter entered the Navy's fleet on February 19, 2005. The $3.2 billion boat was the first submarine named after a living former president.

John Negro Ponte was nominated by George Bush as the U.S. first Director of National Intelligence (DNI) in February 2005.

CIVIL, CIVIC and VIVID are some of the few five-letter words using ONLY Roman Numerals.

American Airlines' AAdvantage miles program was first introduced in 1981 along with frequent-flier miles.

Hertz was the first (February 2005) car rental company to charge a reservation fee. Car rental companies have more fees, taxes and surcharges than airlines, hotels, cruise lines and vacation packages.

"Gone with the Wind" (1939) was the first color movie to win the best picture award.

Lufthansa Airlines recently (February 2005) opened the first terminal in the world where passengers are treated like VIPs. The terminal at Frankfurt Airport is exclusively for airlines first-class and high mileage passengers.

Dallas-born Aaron T-Bone Walker was a classy polished guitarist and vocalist. He was the first great electric blues guitarist, praised by B.B. King and an influence on Chuck Berry, Eric Clapton, Jimi Hendrix and Stevie Ray Vaughn.

First—The Bill Clinton Years

William Jefferson Clinton (Bill Clinton) America's first baby boomer president.

December 18, 1995: Deploys the first 8,000 of some 20,000 troops to Bosnia and 12-month peace keeping mission.

October 29, 1997: Chinese President Jiang Zemin visits Washington for the first U.S.-China summit in eight years.

February 2, 1998: Proposes the first balanced budget in 30 years.

June 27, 1998: Visits China for a summit with Jiang, the first since 1989.

September 30, 1998: Announces the first federal budget surplus since 1969.

October 7, 1999: Urges the Senate to approve the Comprehensive Test Ban Treaty. The Senate rejection is its first of a major treaty supported by a president since 1920.

November 16, 2000: Visits Vietnam, becoming the first president to visit the United States' former enemy since Richard Nixon in 1969.

January 20, 1992: The first president to have his Inaugural Ceremony broadcast over the Internet.

July 21, 2000: Visit to Okinawa will be the first by an American President to Okinawa since the U.S. returned the Southern Japanese Islands to Tokyo's' control.

June 29, 2000: Nominated Norman Nineta to lead the Commerce Department, making the first Asian-American Cabinet Secretary.

February 14, 2000: Receives a life-long achievement award for The League of United Latin American Citizens, the first time the nonpartisan group has honoured a president.

November 21, 1999: Visits Bulgaria, first U.S. President to visit this country in 98 years of bilateral relations.

November 8, 1999: Meet with Quebec separtist Premier Lucien Bouchard, this is a first between an American President and a separtist premier from Quebec, Canada.

Year 1999: Visit to Oglala Sioux nation was the first in 60 years to an Indian Reservation by a president since Franklyn Roosevelt passed through Cherokee country on vacation.

January 2001: Hillary Rodham Clinton, Wife of President Bill Clinton was sworn in as a Junior Senator from New York, thus becoming the first First Lady to win a Senatorial Seat. (But also the first president to be the husband to a U.S. Senator.) This logically follows.

Year: The first sitting president to tour Africa.

January 2000: First time not ONE Supreme Court Justice was present at a State of the Union Address by a U.S. President. Clintons last address.

March 2000: Visit Bangladesh, first time by a U.S. President.

January 1992: Appoints the first female U.S. Attorney General—Janet Reno. Reno served the longest of all U.S. Attorney Generals, 8 years.

Year 1993: Appoints first Black Surgeon General, Dr. Jocelyn Elders. Clinton fired Elders after she said children should be taught about masturbation.

Year 2000: The first visit to India by a U.S. President in 22 years.

Year 1999: Federal Judge in Arkansas ordered Clinton to pay nearly $90,000 to Paula Jones' legal team for giving fake testimony about his relationship with Monica Lewinsky, marking the first time a sitting president has been punished for contempt of court.

September 2000: Shakes hands with Cuba's Fidel Castro at the U.N., the first ever for a sitting U.S. President.

January 1992: Appointed Madeline Albright as the first woman to be Secretary of State.

January 1992 & 1997: One of ONLY 6 presidents to have danced at their inaugurations; the others were George Washington, William Henry Harrison, Lyndon Johnson, Jimmy Carter, Ronald Reagan and George Bush.

January '92-January 2001: ONLY one of seven left-handed presidents to serve two terms. One of ONLY two presidents to be impeached but was never convicted.

January 2001: The Clintons will be the last former president and first lady eligible for Secret Service protection for life.

February 2001" Clinton rents office space in New York City that cost $500,000 per year. He is the first former president to rent office space that's so expensive that it exceeds the rent for all the other former alive presidents combined. Clinton decided to look in Harlem after coming under fierce criticism for trying to rent more expensive space in Manhattan. Rent for the 7,000-square-foot space on 125th Street has been estimated at $210,000 a year.

June 2004" Clinton launched a national book tour in June with the publication of his much-anticipated memoir, "My Life". More than 500,000 copies of the book were sold in its first day of publication, surpassing the all time record set by his wife Hillary's "Living History."

THEY CALLED HIM—"THE FIRST 'BLACK' PRESIDENT".

Pope John Paul II

Pope John Paul was christened Karol Wojtyla. The first Pole ever and first non-Italian Pope in 455 years. Karol graduated first in his class of '44 and in 1938 enrolled on full scholarship in Jagiellonian University, a Catholic College in Krakow, Poland. He is fluent in French, English, Spanish, Greek, Italian, Latin and German. As a Cardinal he made two trips to the United States. The first in 1969 included his first helicopter trip.

On his first papal trip outside Rome, to Assisi on November 5, 1978, he told the cheering crowds that the church "speaks with my voice". John Paul used his first papal trip abroad to Central America in January 1979, to make it plain he disapproved of "Liberation Theology". He visits the Dominican Republic as his first stop.

In October 1979, he made his first papal visit to the United States. Of the six cities he visited one was Philadelphia. John Paul was the first pope to enter a synagogue, the first vicar of Rome to establish formal ties between the Vatican and Israel, the first St. Peter's successors, to publicly acknowledge Jewish religious leaders as spiritual peers.

According to procedures outlined by the Vatican to select a Pope, the Cardinals will first assemble in the Pauline Chapel, decorated with Michelangelo frescoes to Saints Peter and Paul, and sing a Latin hymn, "Veni Creator", which seek guidance from The Holy Spirit. It's almost certain the next Pope will be among the 117 Cardinals eligible to elect John Paul's successor: although technically the Cardinals can select any baptized male Roman Catholic, the last and ONLY time they looked outside their elite group was 1378.

Pope John Paul II was the first Pope to have an audience with a president of the United States at the White House in Washington, D.C.

On October 5, 1991 the Pope prays in St. Peters Basilica with two Lutheran bishops, the first such occasion since the Reformation.

John Paul II the third-longest serving pontiff in history, surpassed ONLY by the first Pope, St. Peter, who served 34 years, and Pius IX, who served 31 years.

There were ONLY two Popes using two names: John Paul I and John Paul II.

"VIVA LA PAPA"

U.S. Navy F-14 pilot Chip King was the first American pilot to fly a mission over Afghanistan and now (2005) is a test pilot for Gulfstream.

Anthony von Leeuwenhoek (1632-1723) was the first scientist to see and draw sperm cells.

Guantanamo Bay is separated from the rest of Cuba by heavily guarded barriers; "Gitmo" is the ONLY U.S. base on hostile territory.

In 1986 the Everly Brothers were the first siblings to be inducted into Rock 'N Roll Hall of Fame.

In the summer of 2004 Emirates Airlines began its first U.S. flights to New York City's JFK airport. It costs Emirates ONLY 8.5 cents to carry one passenger one mile (the cost per available seat mile, or CASM a common industry measurement).

Amina Wadud, an Islamic scholar at Virginia Commonwealth University, and the organizers who invited her claim that she is the first woman (March 2005) to have presided over a mixed-gender prayer service in public since Islam's earliest days.

OxyContin (a potent painkiller drug) first became a problem in Tazewell, Virginia in 1998, but its national reach is well known ensnaring even radio impresario Rush Limbaugh in a scandal that sent him into rehab.

Malcom Bricklin, the auto entrepreneur who brought America, among other automotive disasters, the Yugo will become in 2007 the first American to import cheap cars from China, made by the mainland manufacturer Chery.

Single Integrated Operational Plan (SIOP) has the extra classification Extremely Sensitive Information, used ONLY for our nuke attack plant.

Americans first tried changing times in 1918. Congress finally made clock changes permanent in 1966, but states can opt out.

Meet the Press is the longest running show in television. When it first aired in November 1947 Harry Truman was president.

Dr. Georgeanna Seegar Jones and her husband Dr. Howard Jones established the in-vitro fertilization program at Eastern Virginia Medical School in 1978 in Norfolk. In 1981, the couple announced the birth of Elizabeth Jordon Carr, the country's first baby conceived outside the mother's body.

Supreme Court Judge David Souler, a Rhodes Scholar is the ONLY member of the Supreme Court that has never been married.

Oregon's Death with Dignity Act, twice approved in statewide voter referendums, is the ONLY statute in 2005 in the U.S. allowing doctors to write lethal prescriptions for terminally ill patients who want to control the time and place of their death.

In 1857 Fitz Hugh Ludlow wrote the first popular book about cannabis use, The Hasheesh Eater.

South African President Thabo Mbeki is the first person local and international to be called at the slightest point of trouble, and the one African influence powerful enough to strong-arm rival factions into cease-fires and sometimes even peace deals.

Barack Obama, son of a Black Kenyan, the U.S. Senate: third Black member since Reconstruction grew up in Hawaii and attended Columbia University and Harvard Law School, where he became the first African-American president of The Harvard Law Review.

KEN JENNINGS, A SOFTWARE ENGINEER FROM SALT LAKE CITY, UTAH MADE HISTORY ON JEOPARDY IN 2004. HE BECAME THE FIRST CONTESTANT TO WIN 73 CONSECUTIVE GAMES, THE FIRST PERSON TO WIN $2,520,750 DOLLARS—A RECORD IN THE U.S. FOR ALL GAME SHOWS ON TV. HE LOST BECAUSE HE FAILED TO ANSWER CORRECTLY A QUESTION IN THE CATEGORY: BUSINESS & INDUSTRY__MOST OF THIS FIRM'S 70,000 WHITE-COLLAR EMPLOYEES WORK ONLY 4 MONTHS PER YEAR? THE CORRECT ANSWER WAS

_____.

The end.